CW01476118

Clare of Assisi:
A Living Flame of Love

John O'Brien OFM

Publisher: Bro. John

This book is dedicated to
Bro. Seán Murphy, ofm

Love is reborn in solitude

– Paul Tillich

Contents

List of Abbreviations used 6

Foreword 7

Chapter 1 The Dangling Conversation 9

Chapter 2 A Brief Biography 19

Chapter 3 One With Jesus 33

Chapter 4 The Cross: Love and Acceptance 50

Chapter 5 Clare, a Footprint of Our Lady 61

Chapter 6 Never-ending Song of Love 69

Chapter 7 Do Not Extinguish the Spirit 81

Chapter 8 Journeying into God: The Resumed Conversation 98

Conclusion 107

Epilogue 109

Sources 111

Select Bibliography 112

Abbreviations

1LAg:	1st Letter to Agnes of Prague
2LAg:	2nd Letter
3LAg:	3rd Letter
4LAg:	4th Letter
BC:	Blessing of Saint Clare
FF:	Fonti Francescane
FFr:	Frate Francesco
FSor:	Forma Sororum
LM:	Major Life of Saint Francis
Reg C:	Rule (Form of Life) of Saint Clare
TsC:	The Testament of Saint Clare
TD:	Theodrama
VM:	Vita Minorum

Foreword

I would like to thank Mícheál, Louis and the community of St. Isidore's who made me welcome for my mini-sabbatical. They showed me much kindness. Also I would like to thank Bogdan for his help. I would especially like to thank Professor Allessandra Romagnoli Bartolomei who advised me and directed me to some important papers.

Also I would like to thank Lydia Corbett (formerly Sylvette David) for allowing me to use a copy of her painting of Francis and Clare, from her work with Ann Elison "An Explosion of Love". The icon on the cover is a detail from an icon painted by Domenica Ghidotti. She asks St. Clare to help us understand and sing of love.

Finally a special word of gratitude to Cieran Temple, Linda O'Halloran and all at Temple Printing.

Chapter One

The Dangling Conversation

"The Dangling Conversation"

– Lyrics by Paul Simon

It's a still life water color,
Of a now late afternoon,
As the sun shines through the curtained lace
And shadows wash the room.
And we sit and drink our coffee
Couched in our indifference,
Like shells upon the shore
You can hear the ocean roar
In the dangling conversation
And the superficial sighs,
The borders of our lives.

And you read your Emily Dickinson,
And I my Robert Frost,
And we note our place with bookmarkers
That measure what we've lost.
Like a poem poorly written
We are verses out of rhythm,
Couplets out of rhyme,
In syncopated time
And the dangled conversation
And the superficial sighs,
Are the borders of our lives.

Yes, we speak of things that matter,
With words that must be said,
"Can analysis be worthwhile?"
"Is the theater really dead?"

And how the room is softly faded
And I only kiss your shadow,
I cannot feel your hand,
You're a stranger now unto me
Lost in the dangling conversation.
And the superficial sighs,
In the borders of our lives.

Federico Fellini (+1993) was a famous film director. As a young man he loved the circus and clowns. When he grew older he fell in love with women and married Giuletta Masina (+1993). In a film he released in 1954 called "La Strada" he turned Giuletta into a clown. In the film Giuletta plays a character called Gelsomina. My favourite scene in the film is when Gelsomina and her boss Zampano perform their act at a wedding. The children press Gelsomina to visit a sick child. The child lives in a world of fear and illness. Gelsomina performs her clown act and the child begins to respond. She (Gelsomina) radiates love and loves all. She gives to others what is most denied to herself.

The plot of the film revolves around the two characters - Gelsomina and Zampano. Zampano is played by Anthony Quinn. He is a bully and a brutal man. He is someone who has been brutalised by life and the only way he knows is cruelty and hardness.

He comes upon a family who are suffering hard times. He effectively buys Gelsomina from the family. She is a simple girl. Yet her simplicity is that of a child. She is loving and open to all.

She goes on the road (La Strada) with Zampano. On their adventures they encounter an enemy of Zampano called 'il matto' (the mad one). He is played by Richard Basehart. On the road Gelsomina develops her clown act and with the help of 'il matto' she even composes a piece of music (a theme that runs throughout the film). She confesses to 'Il Matto' that she feels worthless. He consoles her telling her we all belong in some mysterious way. Meanwhile the violence of Zampano increases. Gelsomina refuses to leave because she loves him. He does not reciprocate.

Ultimately, Zampano's violence explodes and he kills 'il matto'. This has the effect of destroying Gelsomina and Zampano leaves her. At the end of the film Zampano is remorseful and comes to look for Gelsomina. He hears a woman humming the tune Gelsomina had composed. He asks where is she, only to find out she is dead. In the final scene he goes to the beach and breaks down and cries. This is the most human act we see in Zampano. He has come to realise that he has lost the only good thing that ever happened in his life.

In an interview Fellini[1] gave he spoke of how his films don't really have an ending. He saw his characters living on somehow in the hope of finding what was denied them in life. He creates an atmosphere about Gelsomina. In the opening scene she is found before the wide open sea. It is as if she is confronting a vast universe in which she does not belong. Her loneliness and rejection by Zampano is shown in little scenes. As he finished his act he accepts the applause – then the camera pans to the solitary Gelsomina, ignored by all. In the scene where Gelsomina meets 'il matto' first she is filmed under a poster speaking of Our Lady. She is like Prince Myshkin in Dostoyevski's 'The Idiot'. He is a truly Christ-like person but in the world he finds himself in is completely out of place. He is the one who is regarded as the idiot while those who destroy themselves and others are regarded as the sane ones. Gelsomina has the same simplicity as the prince.

The film shows us the missed opportunity in Zampano's life. He is one of these people who never received any good thing in life. His heart was blocked to Gelsomina's love and this ultimately kills Gelsomina. It is a story of missed meeting and opportunity. Yet Gelsomina's death forces Zampano to acknowledge his loss, but in acknowledging her loss he has to confront the fact that it is a loss. He was loved and was loved most truly.

The Dangling Conversation

Prayer is where we enter into an I-Thou relationship of love with God. We enter into union with Jesus through the power of the Holy Spirit and

[1]Interview with Vinenzo Mollica, Fellini racconta, videocasetta, De Agostini/Video Rai

we come to God the Father. Our I-Thou with the divine Father is prepared by our relationship with other human beings. The smile of the mother is what brings the response of love of a child (Von Balthasar). This prepares us for meeting others and ultimately leads to our relationship with God.

Our prayer can deepen from vocal prayer to a deeper prayer of the heart. There are different names we can use for the depth-prayer. One is contemplation. Here our heart loves God and God loves us in turn. Here we allow love transform us and in silence I allow heart to speak to heart. The word 'mysticism' can be used for this. The word carries baggage with it in that one associates it with extraordinary phenomena, but it is becoming more normal to think of mysticism in the ordinary (Rahner).

David B. Perrin reflects on the idea of mysticism and this is what he says:

> 'I suggest that the core of mysticism is the radical surrender of self to the loving embrace of the Other who is at the foundation of all life, the One to whom we owe our very existence. This acute awareness may occur with or without the extraordinary phenomena mentioned above. Thus, to enter into the depth of the human experience known as mysticism is to enter into the story of the passionate love affair between humanity and the divine. This outpouring of love has resulted in the transformation of individuals, society, and the church in very many different ways. Some examples will show how this is true.'
> (Mysticism in *The Blackwell Companion to Christian Spirituality*, p. 443)

The idea of radical surrender of self is important. There are many people who are broken. They did not receive the loving smile of a parent. Many have been broken by life and lost the ability to trust. Loneliness can mean that people feel they are nothing and they are nobodies. The world we live in can be cruel and callous. Those who are very ill are often abandoned and left lonelier still. When they hear 'God is love', they feel far removed from the experience.

Those who enter the space of total surrender, the place of the Holy Spirit, do so not just for themselves but they also enter that space so as to give strength to the broken and allow them enter that space. In our look at Fellini's 'La Strada' we saw love denied. Pope Francis gave an interview to Antonino Spadaro (*Osservatore Romano*, 25/9/2013). In it he tells us not to ask people if they are gay or have had an abortion. He uses the image of the medic in a war zone. When people are deeply wounded we do not ask about their cholesterol levels. It is not ours to judge. It is our call to heal by being love to those who are in pain. People like 'Gelsomina' need our love.

Perrin in the above definition of mysticism speaks of our entering the passionate love affair between humanity and the divine. The outpouring of this love is what leads to inner transformation and this is meant to be poured out on others. It is in this context I see Clare as a model and inspiration. She also accompanies mystically those who seek to enter this love affair between the divine and us. Clare surrendered to God and left her heart free for this love. She entered a profound loving relationship with God in love. She takes seriously the words:

> 'That is why I am telling you not to worry about your life and what you are to eat, nor about your body and how you are to clothe it. Surely life means more than food, and the body more than clothing! Look at the birds in the sky. They do not sow or reap or gather into barns; yet your heavenly Father feeds them. Are you not worth much more than they are? Can any of you, for all his worrying, add one single cubit to his span of life? And why worry about clothing? Think of the flowers growing in the fields; they never have to work or spin; yet I assure you that not even Solomon in all his regalia was robed like one of these. Now if that is how God clothes the grass in the field which is there today and thrown into the furnace tomorrow, will he not much more look after you, you men of little faith? So do not worry; do not say, "What are we to eat? What are we to drink? How are we to be clothed?" It is the pagans who set their hearts on all these things. Your heavenly Father knows

you need them all. Set your hearts on his kingdom first, and on his righteousness, and all these other things will be given you as well. So do not worry about tomorrow; tomorrow will take care of itself. Each day has enough trouble of its own.'

(Mt 6:25-34).

This explains Clare and Francis' radical poverty. Their poverty consists in absolute trust in God. They abandon all to his care and providence. For Francis and Clare the love of God is revealed fully in Jesus who gave his life for us (see Gal. 2:20). To enter this love Clare tells Agnes of Prague to look at the mirror of Jesus. In medieval times the mirror could mean paradigm (see Peterson, Clare of Assisi, p. 281). In looking contemplatively at Jesus we see the person we are called to be and we allow his love transform us.

She says to Agnes:
'Place your mind before the mirror of eternity,
Place your soul in the brilliance of glory!
Place your heart in the fragrance of the divine substance,
and through contemplation,
transform your entire being into the image
of the Godhead itself,
so that you too may feel what friends feel
in tasting the hidden sweetness,
that, from the beginning,
God has reserved for his loves.'

(3LAg, P.51 of *The Lady*)

Is Love Possible:

As we saw in the case of Zampano and Gelsomina, so often the reason we do not receive love is because of missed opportunities and hardness of heart. This is the story of many people and organisations. Is love possible? It is easy to believe that it is not possible when we are confronted by the hard things that happen to us.

14

One of the reasons God calls some souls to an alternative way of life in monasteries and convents is to teach us that love in God is possible. Clare and Francis are two of those chosen people. They reflect to us that love is possible. They were friends and influenced each other. Antoine De-Saint Exupery once said that love doesn't consist in looking into each other's eyes, but in looking together in the same direction. Both were in love with God in Christ and this was the source of their spiritual friendship.

In the Gospel of Luke we read: 'Be compassionate as your Holy Father is compassionate.' (Lk 6:36). Mercy and compassion are the faces that love wears. Clare and Francis experienced this loving kindness and radiated it to others. One could say they dared to be happy in this love. In the First Letter of Saint John we read that if 'anybody says he is without sin, he deceives himself' (1 Jn 1:8). This is true of Francis and Clare but their happiness rests in the fact they are forgiven, accepted, loved and become new people in God.

In the first letter of Saint John we also read: 'Behold, let us love one another, because love is from God: anyone who loves is born of God and knows God' (1 Jn 4:7). Then he goes on to say, 'God's love was revealed among us in this way: "God sent his only son among us so that we might love through him".' (1 Jn 4:9). Clare and Francis lived in the atmosphere of love in the Holy Spirit. This love was the reason they abandoned all and lived in God by the power of the Holy Spirit. They allowed this love transform them. Their prayer was the prayer of Mary: 'Let it be done to me according to your word.' (Lk 1:38). Clare wrote to Agnes of Prague telling her of gaining him who gave all so that we could have life (see 3LAg7). John tells us in his letter: 'Beloved, since God loved us so much, we ought to love one another. No-one has ever seen God: if we love one another, God lives in us and we in God' (1 Jn 4:11f). The revelation of love is Jesus the Christ. By living in love and contemplating love we live in God. Clare and Francis' witness to this and their witness is an indicator to us to draw inspiration for our journey into God. In this work I concentrate on Clare rather than Francis. Her part has been re-discovered in many modern studies. Pope Benedict

XVI wrote an encyclical called 'Deus Caritas Est' (God is love). One of his aims in writing the letter was to emphasise what is at the heart of our belief. We are called to enter into the heart of love and from that place bring the love to others. The witness of holy people shows us this is possible. Pope John Paul II said that 'we have to reconstruct our interior world, a world that is inspired and sustained by the Holy Spirit. This reconstruction is reached by prayer and by reaching out to others. In this way we can continue to the healing of the illnesses of our times.' (see Zenini, *Enciclopedio della Preghiera*, p.131). The illnesses of our time include loneliness, addictions, meaninglessness and many people (like Gelsomina) feeling they are worthless. In looking towards God in prayer we discover our true identity and then we find our true selves. Clare and Francis lived in this way. Pope Francis spoke of the joy discovering God's love in Jesus (Evangelii Gaudium). We can abandon ourselves into the hands of the one who loves us truly. Jesus tells us, 'I am with you always: yes to the end of time' (Mt 28:20). In this lies our hope.

Silent Loving

St. Francis received the marks of the crucified Jesus on his own body when he was on retreat on Mount La Verna. He was very ill at this stage and he stayed in a little hut near San Damiano. He was looked after by Clare and her ladies. (see *Legend of Three Companions*, 83-84). Women are often more sensitive than men when it comes to illness and one can understand why the jaded and ill St. Francis decided to stay here. In his pain, he composed a beautiful canticle in praise of God:

'Most High, all-powerful, good Lord,
Yours are the praises, the glory, the honour, and all blessing.
To you alone, Most High, do they belong,
and no human is worthy to mention Your name.
Praised be You, my Lord, with all Your creatures,
especially Sir Brother Sun,
Who is the day and through whom You give us light.
And he is beautiful and radiant with great splendour;
and bears a likeness of You, Most High One.

Praised be You, my Lord, through Sister Moon and the stars,
in heaven You formed them clear and precious and beautiful.
Praised be You, my Lord, through Brother Wind,
and through the air, cloudy and serene, and every kind of
weather,
through which you give sustenance to Your creatures.
Praised be You, my Lord, through our Sister Mother Earth,
who sustains and governs us,
and who produces varied fruits with coloured flowers and
herbs.
Praised be You, my Lord, through those who give pardon for
Your love,
and bear infirmity and tribulation.
Blessed are those who endure in peace
for by You, Most High, shall they be crowned.
Praised be You, my Lord, through our Sister Bodily Death,
from whom no one living can escape.
Woe to those who die in mortal sin.
Blessed are those whom death will find in Your most holy
will,
for the second death shall do them no harm.
Praise and bless my Lord and give Him thanks
and serve Him with great humility.'

He leaves San Damiano with his so-called "Exhortation to Saint Clare
and her Sisters". On one level one could think that we might say Clare
is not present. Yet when we reflect on Clare's life we see her spirit
permeates the two canticles! Francis was influenced by Clare's
friendship.

'Listen, little poor ones called by the Lord,
who have come together from many parts and provinces.
Live always in truth,
that you may die in obedience.
Do not look at the life outside,
for that of the Spirit is better.

'I beg you through great love,
to use with discretion
the alms which the Lord gives you.

'Those who are weighed down by sickness
and the others who are wearied because of them,
all of you: bear it in peace.
For you will sell this fatigue at a very high price
and each one [of you] will be crowned queen
in heaven with the Virgin Mary.'

Chapter 2

A Brief Biography

In the first half of the thirteenth century, Assisi was a small town of medium importance. It is situated in the heart of the Umbrian valley and knew all the ups and downs of the duchy of Spoleto, following the death of Henry VI. There was continual tension between the emperor Frederick II and the Popes. Together they made Central Italy, and especially Umbria, their battleground. As the century wore on the merchant class became increasingly important. Clare's family, unlike that of Francis, did not come from the newly emerging class. On the contrary, she was a member of the Maiores, the nobles and ruling class. At the bottom of the ladder were the minores, the poor, outcasts and those who served the Maiores and the new merchant class, to which Francis' father belonged.

After the first Crusades in 1096 and the ones that followed, knightly chivalry and romantic stories of heroic knights were very influential. Francis at a young age wished to leave the merchant class and become a knight. Assisi, at this time, had become more urbanised. Clare's father was a knight (called a *miles*) and belonged to the descendants of Offreduccio. The head of the clan was Clare's uncle, Monaldo. After him came Favarone, then the other brothers, each of whom had their own estate and family. Clare's mother was Ortoluna and she is one who played a large part in Clare's life. She had gone on many pilgrimages, including Compostella and the Holy Land. She made an important pilgrimage to Mont Gargano - important for our story. There was a special shrine there to St. Michael. As she prayed before the cross there, she heard an inner voice telling her:

'You will give birth to a light that will shine brilliantly in the world' (Proc 3:28). Ortoluna was afraid of childbirth as she was pregnant, but she gave birth to Clare in 1193. Historians quibble about the year and date of her birth (see Cremaschi, Chiara di Assisi, p.195f). Clare's name in Italian is Chiara and refers to radiance of light. Ortoluna remembered the prophecy in Gargano and named her daughter Chiara accordingly. Clare is the english form of 'Chiara'.

There was tension between the Maiores and the new merchant class and this erupted into war. The Rocco Maggiore castle was attacked. The Maiores left Assisi and formed an alliance with their old enemies in Perugia. Francis and Clare's family found themselves on opposite sides. At the battle of Collestada (1202) Francis was taken prisoner. He experienced illness, loneliness and a questioning of the world he had found. His father rescued him after a year.

Francis' Conversion

Francis was a victim of war. He had seen human cruelty and broken bodies and broken minds. He still, however, hankered after glory, pomp and power. Walter of Brienne wanted to take control of the great fiefs in Apulia, a distant and rugged part of Italy, that Walter claimed belonged to his wife. Count Gentile hoped to join Walter and Francis joined Gentile. However, on the road he had a dream. He was ushered in to a beautiful place upon hearing his name; the place was filled with shining shields and other arms. He was asked to serve the master and not the servant. He later had a dream in which he was told to return home.

When he returned home he was beginning to change even more. Once he had been a party animal and the king of the revellers. He still worked in his father's shop selling cloth, but quite often he would give the proceeds to the poor. This would lead to a break with his father. He would retire to lonely places and caves and pray there.

At the same time he brought a friend with him who remained outside while Francis prayed. This man was one Francis loved more than all the rest (1 Cel 3). This man's quiet sacrifice was crucial to Francis, because as Francis changed he helped him keep his sanity and he was overjoyed to see Francis become radiant with joy in the Holy Spirit. His name is lost to us. His sacrifice of himself helped Francis grow.

One of the places St. Francis prayed in was the ruined church of San Damiano. Here he had a truly mystical experience. He heard a voice from the crucifix which said to him: 'Do you not see, Francis, that my house is crumbling? Go, then, and repair it for me' (Manselli, St. Francis of Assisi, p.54). Manselli sees the testimony of the *'Legend of the Three Companions'* as being more reliable rather than the first Life of Celeno. In hearing the voice from the cross he truly believed it was Christ who spoke to him. The crucifix at San Damiano made Francis aware of the suffering of Christ as a superhuman reality in the reality of human existence. It was the only thing that could give meaning to human suffering. The cross showed Jesus' communion and compassion with the poor and broken. Francis thought that the church referred to in the voice referred to San Damiano and he set about repairing the little church there. One day while riding on his horse in the area around Assisi he met a leper. Lepers repelled Francis but now he was changing. He forced himself to embrace the leper. He says in his testament:

> 'The Lord gave me, Brother Francis, thus to begin doing penance in this way: for when I was in sin, it seemed too bitter for me to see lepers. And the Lord Himself led me among them and I showed mercy to them. And when I left them, what had seemed bitter to me was turned into sweetness of soul and body. And afterwards I delayed a little and left the world.'
>
> (Testament in *The Founder*, p.124).

He was no longer a rich merchant but a reject among rejects. He had made a choice to leave the world he knew and embrace the world of the Spirit.

Francis continued to sell cloth to fund his rebuilding of San Damiano. His father lost it and demanded recompense from Francis. He brought the case to the bishop. Francis stripped himself and gave away everything, saying that he had only one Father, God in heaven. The bishop clothed Francis and he had begun a new way of life. He continued to beg for stones and help to rebuild the church. The king of the revellers was different. He became a laughing stock initially and experienced much rejection. Gradually people began to sense this man was sincere and a genuine man of prayer. Gradually others joined him. He did not wish to fall away as had the Cathars and other groups. He went to Rome and got approval for his new movement. His new movement was recognised. Manselli tells us that Francis was to assume the part of the one who was nothing and had nothing (St. Francis of Assisi, p.62). He sought to be one with Christ in reaching out to those who were thought of as nothing. He and his new community tended to the lepers and bound up their wounds. Instead of condemning others in the church such as the monks and clergy, Francis sought to be authentic himself and around him like-minded souls began to gather.

Clare and Francis Meet

Over the years Clare grew into a beautiful young woman. One of the witnesses at her canonisation process, Lord Ranierio de Bernardo of Assisi, lets us know this. Clare's family returned to Assisi around 1210. It was here she first heard Francis preach. Already Clare and her family were living a life of prayer and practical charity (see Peterson, Clare of Assisi, p.91-93). Francis came to know of Clare and her holiness. Ingrid Peterson tells us they met and discussed a new form of life (Clare of Assisi, p.105 f).

On Palm Sunday, March 18, 1212 when the people of Assisi were at mass, Clare remained in her seat and the bishop came to her. He gave her a palm branch. This was a symbolic gesture suggesting her renunciation of the social conventions of the time with its longing for wealth. It was an invitation to her to follow the suffering Christ. This was the time she left her home and met Francis at the little church of St. Mary of the Angels where she had her hair cut and she gave herself to God after the example of Francis. The symbolism of the cutting of her hair showed her radical surrender. She was a beautiful young woman.

Her family were furious and wondered what was this madness. Francis brought Clare to St. Angelo di Panzo. Her family tried to convince her to return but to no avail (Leg C9; Proc 18:3). Here sister Caterina came to join her. This time the leader of the family, Monaldo, thought it was time to take a firmer stand. He brought a group of knights with him, but Caterina, who was now Sr. Agnes, was too strong physically for Monaldo and his knights. She felt a great strength in the Holy Spirit. Monaldo tried to strike her with his sword but he was unable to move (Leg C 25). Monaldo and his knights withdrew in confusion. Eventually Clare and her sister came to the church of San Damiano, the church Francis had rebuilt. There Clare said God the Father illuminated her heart through Francis. She was illuminated by the light of the Spirit (Test C 24-32). Here she began her silent dialogue with the divine Thou. She wished to emulate the Christ who was poor and embrace him (see 2L Ag, 18-20).

In the sixth chapter of her Form of Life, her rule, Clare relates how Francis kept an eye on the small but growing community and when he saw they had no fear of poverty, hard work, trial or shame, but instead held them as great delights, he provided them with a "Form of Life".

> ...Because by divine inspiration you have made yourselves daughters and handmaids of the most High, most exalted King, the heavenly Father, and have taken the Holy Spirit as your spouse, choosing to live according to the perfection of the holy Gospel, I resolve and promise for myself and for my brothers always to have the same loving care and special solicitude for you as for them.

Shortly before his death, Francis wrote another expression of his hope for Clare and her companions:

> I, little brother Francis, wish to follow the life and poverty of our most high Lord Jesus Christ and of His most holy Mother and to persevere in this until the end; and I ask you, my ladies, and I give you my advice that you live always in this most holy life and poverty. And keep careful watch that you never depart from this by reason of the teaching or advice of anyone.

Its simplicity is once more quite striking. There is, nevertheless, a prophetic sense contained in its words, one that was undoubtedly inspired by a realisation that the boldness of Clare's vision of a Gospel life in poverty would be tested over and over again.

There are no other extant documents of either Francis or Clare that provide more details concerning their daily life in those first years. In his *Historia orientalis et occidentalis*, Jacques de Vitry, an astute observer of new forms of religious life at that time, described the life of the Lesser Brothers and Sisters in 1216. The French ecclesiastic writes initially in general terms: "They live according to the form of the primitive Church... go into the cities and villages during the day... but return to their hermitages or solitary places at night, employing themselves in contemplation." Then, undoubtedly prompted by his interest in the feminine religious movements, he proceeds to focus his attention. "The women," he writes, "live near the cities in various hospices. They accept nothing, but live from the work of their hands. In fact, they are very much offended and disturbed because they are honoured by the clergy and laity more than they deserve." Was de Vitry describing Clare and her sisters? It is difficult to determine but it is likely he referred to Clare and her sisters. (see *The Lady*, p.10f).

Around this time there were a number of movements of women who adopted lives of prayer and penance. Some were women who were attached to individual churches. After the Lateran Council of 1215 there began a move to organise these into communities under the rule of St. Benedict.

Clare, however, had her own privilege of poverty and she was under the influence of St. Francis. By now the community of San Damiano was growing and Francis asked Clare to become abbess of the new community. She refused initially but St. Francis pressed her and she conceded to his request. This was in 1216. Two years later Pope Honorius appointed Hugolino dei Conti di Segni as protector of Clare and her sisters. Hugolino gave exemptions and privileges to Clare and the sisters of San Damiano. Hugolino tried to bring stability and protection by introducing his own detailed and austere "Form of Life" based on St. Benedict. He was nervous, always, about the privilege of poverty. He admired Clare immensely but he questioned could anyone live in poverty depending on providence for their needs.

Clare and Fasting:

Caroline Walter Bynum in her opus, *'Holy Feast and Holy Fast'*, looks at the way medieval women who spearheaded the new movements in the church, looked upon food. She looks at the idea of asceticism and the creativity and character of medieval women. Clare took fasting extremely seriously and took this as an indispensable part of her prayer-life. However, Francis and Guido, the local bishop, moderated Clare's fast (Leg C,11). Other food motifs are important in Clare's story as well. She shed tears before the holy food of the Eucharist and approached it with awe (Leg C,19). In 1227 Hugolino became Pope, and took the name Gregory IX. In 1230 he forbade the friars to preach to Clare and her sisters without papal approval.

Clare let it be known that if the pope forbade preachers to come to give them spiritual food then the sisters would refuse to eat the bread provided by the begging brothers (Leg C,23). The pope compromised and the sisters kept their preachers. There was no hunger-strike.

During the process of canonisation the following dream of Clare was mentioned. Clare saw Francis in a vision and took him a jug of hot water and a towel. When she reached him he gave her his breast and gave her suck (Proc 3:29, 6:13). This image seems strange to us, but among medieval women Jesus was seen as mother. Clare's vision means that Francis led Clare to the person of Jesus. Jesus was the source of nourishment and life.

Prayer-life of Clare

Clare accepted the rule of Hugolino but continued to negotiate and modify his rule. It would take the rest of her life before she could make poverty a part of her rule. Until then she had the privilege of poverty. Meanwhile in San Damiano, Clare and her sisters led a life of prayer and contemplation. In her first letter to Agnes of Prague she reminds Agnes to look upon him who became 'contemptible' for us. She did not give many intellectual or practical formulae for making progress in the life of prayer. Clare wanted to teach her sisters that prayer was a matter of falling and remaining in love, a process that defies plans, methods or well-defined approaches. Prayer-life develops when we focus our attention on the Thou of God. In her second letter to Agnes she says: "O most noble queen, gaze, consider, contemplate, as you desire to imitate your Spouse."

Clare's continuous pursuit of a prayer centered on Christ, then, enables us to appreciate why she held poverty in such regard. She realised that a life lived without anything of one's own, frees us to enter into the mystery of God and his kingdom. In her first letter to Agnes of Prague she says: "O Blessed poverty who bestows eternal life on those who love and embrace her! O holy poverty, to those who possess and desire you God promises the kingdom of heaven, and offers instead eternal glory and blessed life." Clare's vision came from her contemplation of Jesus and his life. He was the one who was placed poor in the crib, lived poor in the world and died on the cross. To gaze upon that "mirror" is to embrace his state of being without anything of his own. In her Testament she tells us how St. Francis taught her the inner meaning of poverty. She would often refer to herself as the 'pianticella' (little flower) of St. Francis. In her rule Clare reiterated her teaching about poverty. Clare's poverty showed her trust and faith in the kindness of God and the goodness of people. Her life showed her trust and faith were well founded. She remained close to God and seeing the good in others allowed them to respond.

Clare's prayers were efficacious. In the process of canonisation many healings were attributed to Clare. She performed works of wonder in feeding her community and in all things she gave glory to God. There are two events that show how remarkable her intercession was.

In 1240 Assisi was attached by mercenaries, called Saracens, of the emperor. San Damiano was attacked. Sister Francesca gives the following account of what happened:

> 'Asked what she saw in her, she replied one time, when the Saracens entered the cloister of the said monastery, the

Lady made them bring her to the entrance of the refectory and bring a small box where there was the Blessed Sacrament of the Body of our Lord Jesus Christ. Throwing herself prostrate on the ground in prayer, she begged with tears, saying among other things: "Lord, look upon these servants of yours, because I cannot protect them." Then the witness heard a voice of wonderful sweetness: "I will always defend you!" The Lady then prayed for the city, saying: "Lord, please defend the city as well!" The same voice resounded and said: "The city will endure many dangers, but it will be defended."

Then the Lady turned to the sisters and told them: "Do not be afraid, because I am a hostage for you so that you will not suffer any harm now nor any other time as long as you wish to obey God's commandments." Then the Saracens left in such a way that they did not do any harm or damage.'

(Proc 9:2).

We know this account to be true. In the following year Assisi was besieged by Vitale di Aversa. This time San Damiano was not attacked. Clare and the sisters did penance and the siege was suddenly lifted (Proc 9:3; 3:19; 13:9). Was it because the deposed minister general - Br. Elias - was with the emperor? He was a friend of Clare. We do not know. But we do know Assisi survived. Clare never emphasised the miraculous. She was in union with Jesus and trusted God the Father to act in whatever he saw best.

The last days of St. Francis

From 1224 illness would play a major part in the life of St. Clare. She was very ill in 1224, but recovered, but gradually she would become more and more ill and have to spend more time away from the community. In the same time Francis was exhausted and ill. He went to La Verna to pray and there he received the marks of the stigmata, the wounds of Christ. When he returned to Assisi he had a little hut built for him beside San Damiano. St. Clare, by now a little recovered, nursed him with the sisters. Women in general are more sensitive than men, and in the care of the vulnerable, such as the sick or children, are often kinder. Kindness and care marked Clare as a person and in this vulnerable time in Francis' life, this was what he needed. Here he wrote his "Canticle of the Creatures", as we saw.

In 1226 he returned to the Portiuncula where he passed away. Clare and Francis had explored new ways of being in the church and following God. They had moments of doubt, uncertainty and fear. Yet their friendship helped them through. At times this friendship was in silence - but it was a silence where the Spirit of love was and in whom they were united. The passing of Francis was a great sorrow for Clare and her sisters. As Francis was being led to his resting place he arranged one final farewell.

And How He was Buried with Praise and Glory

"His brothers and sons had assembled with the whole multitude of people from the neighbouring cities, rejoicing to take part in such solemn rites. They spent that entire night of the holy father's death in the praises of God. The sweet sound of jubilation and the brightness of the lights made it seem that angels were keeping vigil.

When day was breaking, the multitude of the city of Assisi gathered with all the clergy. They lifted his sacred body from the place where he had died and carried it with great honour to the city, singing hymns and praises with trumpets blaring. They all took branches of olive and other trees and solemnly followed the funeral procession, bringing even more candles as they sang songs of praise in loud voices.

With the sons carrying their father and the flock following the shepherd who was hastening to the Shepherd of them all, he arrived at the place where he first planted the religion

and the Order of the consecrated virgins and Poor Ladies.
They laid him out in the church of San Damiano, home to
those daughters he gained for the Lord. The small window
was opened, the one used by these servants of Christ at the
appointed time to receive the sacrament of the Lord's body.
The coffin was also opened: in it lay hidden the treasure of
supercelestial powers; in it he who had carried many was
now carried by a few.

The Lady Clare!
Clearly a woman of true brilliance and holiness,
the first mother of all the others,
the first plant of that holy Order;
she comes with her daughters
to see the father
who would never again
speak to them or return to them,
as he was quickly going away.
They looked upon him,
groaning and weeping with great anguish of heart."
(1 Cel 116-117 in the Founder, p.284f).

In their loss, Clare and her sisters found solace in the tender love of God
– who looked after them as a mother.

The growth of the order and a new rule:

Clare's influence began to spread and the number of followers increased
all over Europe. In Prague she came to influence an important personage
called Agnes. She felt called to follow God closely. Ingrid Peterson
gives us the following background to Agnes:

Agnes was born in 1205, a princess of Bohemia, to King
Ottocar I and Queen Constance of Hungary, a relative of
Saint Elizabeth. According to her rank, she was educated by
the Cistercians and betrothed to Frederick II, Emperor of

Germany. Like Clare, Agnes had made a private vow of virginity and could not be persuaded to marry the king. Although incensed because of her rejection, King Frederick is said to have remarked: "If she had left me for a mortal man, I would have taken vengeance with a sword, but I cannot take offense because in preference to me she has chosen the King of Heaven."

(Peterson, Clare of Assisi, P.164f).

In 1232 Agnes obtained property to build a hospice which she later turned over to the Crosiers of the Red Star. She became attracted to the form of life of Clare and the sisters in San Damiano. Clare sent five sisters from the Trent area to help her begin. Agnes and Clare never met, but a correspondence built up between them. We have copies of Clare's letter to Agnes, but none from Agnes to Clare. Agnes, following Clare, wished to live poorly. Clare encouraged her. She said:

"You have rejected all these things and have chosen with your whole heart and soul a life of holy poverty and destitution. Thus you took a spouse of a more noble lineage, Who will keep Your virginity ever unspotted and unsullied, the Lord Jesus Christ."

(1Lag 6-7).

Agnes petitioned Pope Gregory IX for the privilege of poverty, but again he was nervous, hoping they would get income from the hospice. However, after a while, he relented and Agnes handed over the running of the hospice to the Crosiers of the Red Star.

Clare continued to battle all her life to have her way of life recognised. After the death of Gregory a new Pope called Innocent IV came to the throne. He tried to write a more modified form of the Hugolino rule, but Clare was not happy because poverty was not written into the rule.

In 1253 Pope Innocent called on Clare and they discussed the matter. Clare herself wrote a rule for her sisters and before she died she heard that Pope Innocent had approved their rule and way of life. This fact is startling in itself because Clare was the first woman to write a rule in the history of the church. This came at a time when women were considered inferior to men - even Aquinas thought this. I don't think Clare or Agnes ever bothered with this view of women. Alessandra Bartholomei Romognoli, in an article entitled, 'Clausura e Silenzio'[1], shows, after examining the rule, how enclosure (as Clare understood it) and silence were part and parcel of their way of life.

Clare's Last Days:

Agnes, Clare's sister, returned to San Damiano as Clare grew weaker. She came back to care for her. For Clare, prayer for the sick was very important. On Christmas day in 1252, Clare was alone and felt sad she could not attend the Christmas mass. Suddenly she had a vision of the mass and she could hear the music, the singing and the mass. (Proc 3:30 see also FF 3014, FF 3049). Clare became patroness of television because of this.

Just before her death Clare told the sisters to pray. Agnes, her sister, began to pray the prayer of the Five Wounds of Jesus. The last words Clare said to her were: "Precious in the sight of the Lord is the death of his holy ones" (Proc 10:10). Another witness at Clare's death, sister Benvenuta, said: "It seemed in that thought that the heavenly court was moving, and preparing to honour the holy woman. Our most glorious Lady, the Blessed Virgin Mary, was especially preparing some of her garments for the new saint" (Proc 11:14). Benvenuta was here speaking of a vision she and Clare had in Clare's final moments. She had kept it secret until the canonisation process. She had heard earlier Saint Clare make the following statement:

> '...not speaking to any one person, (Clare) began to commend her soul by saying, "Go in peace, because you

[1] Alessandra Bartholomei Romagnol: 'Claura e Silenzio' - the draft of the original article was e-mailed to me by the author. It was a talk given to the Poor Clares of Fora Sabina in 2012. (The acts of the convention were not published at time of writing.) For further discussion see P. Maranesi, La Clausura di Chiara d'Assisi, Assisi 2012.

will have a good escort. The One Who created you has already provided that you will be made holy. The One Who created you has infused the Holy Spirit in you and then guarded you as a mother does her littlest child".' (Proc 113)

It was only in hindsight she realised that Clare was speaking of her soul. When she saw the vision with Clare she realised what Clare's words meant:

(Benvenuta) suddenly saw with her own eyes a great multitude of virgins, all dressed in white with crowns on their heads, coming and entering through the door of that room where the holy mother Clare was lying. Among these virgins there was one greater, above and beyond what could be described, far more beautiful than all the others, and wearing a crown upon her head larger than all the others. Above her crown she had a golden cluster in the form of a white thurible from which such brilliance came forth it seemed to illuminate the entire house. These virgins approached the bed of holy Lady Clare. That virgin who seemed greater at first covered her bed with the most delicate cloth so fine that even though she was covered with it, Lady Clare nonetheless saw through its great delicacy. Then the virgin of virgins, who was greater, inclined her face above the virgin Saint Clare, or above her breast, so that the witness could not discern one from the other. After this was done, they all disappeared. (Proc 11:4).

Clare passed away on August 11th, 1253.

Chapter 3

One With Jesus

In the "Legend of St. Clare" we read that the "beloved crucified took possession of the lover, and she was inflamed with such love of the mystery of the Cross that the power of the Cross is shown by signs and miracles" (Leg C, 3,2 p.308 *The Lady*). The Cross of San Damiano before which St. Francis prayed and heard the voice asking him to go and repair my church was the cross Clare saw every day (2 Cel 10; FF p.593). Francis was transformed in love as he contemplated the love of the one who endured death "for us." Saint Bonaventure describes the transformation in St. Francis in the following words:

> True piety,
> which according to the Apostle
> gives power to all things,
> had so filled Francis's heart
> and penetrated its depths
> that it seemed to have claimed the man of God
> completely into its dominion.
> This is what, through devotion, lifted him up into God;
> through compassion, transformed him into Christ;
> through self-emptying, turned him to his neighbour;
> through universal reconciliation with each thing,
> refashioned him to the state of innocence.
>   (Major Life in *The Founder* p.586).

Led by the Spirit Francis and Clare saw with the eyes of the heart the love Jesus had for all of us. Inflamed by the Holy Spirit they become "prayer" and in union with Jesus become compassionate to all God's people and God's world. The union of Francis and Clare was one of silent worship and contemplation of the crucified one. They become full persons in their own way by "looking together in the same direction." St. Clare tells Agnes of Prague in her second letter:

"If you suffer with Him, you will reign with Him,
weeping with Him, you will rejoice with Him;
dying on the cross of tribulation with Him
you will possess heavenly union with Him
among the splendour of the saints..."

(The Lady, p.49)*.

And in the third letter she says: "May you totally love Him Who gave Himself totally for your love" *(The Lady*, p.51). It is by looking unto Jesus in love that the one who prays is transformed into the beloved. This is the secret of Clare's "mirror" image that she uses when she writes to Agnes. In the Legend of Saint Clare we get an insight into Clare's profound union with Jesus in love. As she prayed she was one with Jesus in his agony:

> Once, the day of the most sacred Supper arrived, in which the Lord loved His own until the end. Near evening, as the agony of the Lord was approaching, Clare, sad and afflicted, shut herself up in the privacy of her cell. While in her own prayer she was accompanying the praying Saviour and when saddened even to death she experienced the effect of His sadness, she was filled at once with the memory of His capture and of the whole mockery and she sank down on her bed. All that night and the following day, she was so absorbed that she remained out of her senses. She seemed to be joined to Christ and to be otherwise totally insensible always focusing the light of her eyes on one thing.
>
> (Leg C in *The Lady*, p.307).

She was inflamed by the rising flame of love that is the Holy Spirit. She shared with Jesus in his prayer for the healing of all humankind. In this brief passage we see the whole life of Clare in an instant. She, like Francis, lived in the presence of Jesus by the Spirit and her life was consumed with the living flame of love. She radiated this to others. This is why so many people came to her for comfort and healing. There was no discrimination amongst those who came to Clare – rich and poor alike all received a gracious welcome. She saw in all of them the figure of Jesus and even though the image of Jesus was sometimes broken, she loved even more. The power of her love brought new life to those who sought her out.

Angela of Foligno (1248-1309) who was canonised in 2013 is another interesting case. She had a conversion experience in which she changed her way of life and became a Franciscan Tertiary. Under the direction of her spiritual director, she recorded her spiritual journey and he published this in the "Memoriale" and "Instructions". She describes in her the way to transformation.

> The first transformation is when the soul attempts to imitate the works of the suffering God-man because in them God's will is and was manifested. The second transformation is when the soul is united to God and has great feelings and great delights from God which still can be conceived or expressed in words. The third transformation is when the soul is transformed within God and God within the soul by a most perfect union. It feels and tastes the highest matters of God to such an extent that they cannot be conceived or expressed in words.
>
> (Instructiones 2 - ed. 412.34 - 414.41).

She experienced deeply the love of God in Jesus and once she cried out "...Love, still unknown, Why? Why? Why?" (Memoriale 3, ed. 178-80).

As Angela grew in love she describes a state of prayer in which she experiences Jesus' loneliness and agony. She describes in the Memonale how she felt "like a person blindfolded with his hands bound behind him, and hung by the neck from a rope, yet remaining alive on the gallows, without aid or any kind of effort or rescue" (Memoriale 8 ed. 338. 21-25). In this state she has all her old vices revive, Angela raged against herself beating and punishing her body and calling out to Jesus "My, my son, do not abandon me" (Memoriale 8, ed. 340.54 cf Matt 27:46). This form of sharing in the abandonment of Christ was Angela's mission. Finally in the Memoriale Angela shows how this dark night gives way to a new dawn (Memoriale ed. 378-92). She describes the joy of being immersed in the trinity and sharing in their sphere of love. Angela gathered other people around her and she was active in caring for the sick, the poor, and anybody in need. Her contemplation overflowed into compassion for all and the need to tend to the wounds of the broken.

Two Modern Spiritual Friends

Hans Urs Von Balthasar (1905-1988) became one of the most important voices of twentieth century theology. He did not see theology as an academic exercise – he deplored the gap that had developed between theology and living in God. He was born in Lucerne in Switzerland. His childhood was pervaded by music, for which he had an extraordinary talent. He would later share this gift with his friend, the protestant theologian Karl Barth. His early studies oscillated between literature and music. One of the people who influenced him during his studies was Rudolf Allers, a one-time disciple of Freud. Allers found his way from psychoanalysis to medieval philosophy and theology. "Opponent of Freud and free disciple of Alfred Adler, he possessed and imported the feeling for interhuman love as the objective medium of human existence; in this turn from the 'ego' to the reality of the full 'Thou' lay for him philosophical thought and psychotherapeutic method." (Von Balthasar, Rechenschaft 1965, p. 34). He completed his doctorate in literature there.

In the summer of 1927 he did a retreat given by Fr. Friedrick Kronseder, S.J. and he received a powerful message:

> Even now, thirty years later, I could still go to that remote path in the Black Forest, not far from Basel, and find again the tree beneath which I was struck as by lightning... And yet it was neither theology nor the priesthood which then came into my mind in a flash. It was simply this: you have nothing to choose, you have been called. You will not serve, you will be taken into service. You have no plans to make, you are just a little stone in a mosaic which has long been ready. All I needed to do was "leave everything and

follow", without making plans, without wishes or insights. All I needed to do was to stand there and wait and see what I would be needed for.

(*Pourquoi je me suis fait prêtre*, p.21)

He entered the Society of Jesus – the Jesuits – and began his studies.

The dry nature of theology shocked him. The riches of the faith were being denied to the students. His sharp mind led him on his own theological quest. He describes his experience as follows:

> My entire period of study in the Society was a grim struggle with the dreariness of theology, with what men had made out of the glory of revelation. I could not endure this presentation of the Word of God. I could have lashed out with the fury of a Samson. I felt like tearing down, with Samson's strength, the whole temple and burying myself beneath the rubble. But it was like this because, despite my sense of vocation, I wanted to carry out my own plans, and was living in a state of unbounded indignation. I told almost no one about this. Przywara understood everything; I did not have to say anything. Otherwise there was no one who could have understood me. I wrote the "Apocalypse" with a dogged determination, resolved, whatever the cost, to rebuild the world from its foundations. It really took Basel, especially the all-soothing goodness of the commentary on St. John, to lead my aggressive will into true indifference.
>
> (cf Von Speyr, Erde und Himmel, p.195).

However, he lived with Henri de Lubac in Lyon who opened for him the treasure of the Fathers. In addition he was friendly with Erich Przywara who taught him so much. On July 26, 1936, Von Balthasar was ordained a priest in his beloved Jesuit order. He did not wish to teach theology at the Gregorian University in Rome, so he became a student chaplain in Basel in Switzerland. Here he came to know Karl Barth and the friendship and dialogue between the two proved fruitful not just for the two men but for all the people whose lives they enriched.

Here, too, he came to know a doctor called Adrienne Von Speyr (+1968). Adrienne was born in 1902 in La Chaux-de-Fonds in Switzerland. She was born in a Protestant family and as a young girl she had many religious questions. Her mother would complain that Adrienne would end up becoming a Catholic one day. Adrienne's relationship with her mother in the early years was not good and after the death of her grandfather followed shortly afterwards by the death of her father, Adrienne went in to herself and felt depressed. She was very attached to the two men. Adrienne became suicidal but she decided not to take her life but give her life for God, no longer to live for herself (Von Speyr, *Dalla mia vita*, p.142). She did become a doctor but in 1918 she became very ill and had to recuperate in the mountains of Switzerland. This was a time of grace for her and the people she met helped her in every way. One day she entered a catholic church and suddenly felt she belonged (Von Balthasar, *Erster Blick*, p.22), but this would take a while longer. She moved to Basel to practice medicine. She was very kind to her patients and she had a great affection for the mentally afflicted. She prayed for them and loved them back to life. In truth she did this for all her patients. She married Emil Dürr but he died tragically in 1934. This was a hard time for Adrienne and she tried to say the words "Thy will be done" but this was an effort. It was a hard and lonely time for Adrienne. She did marry Werner Kaegi in 1936.

In 1940 she had a serious heart condition. She had heard about the new chaplain in Basel, Hans Urs Von Balthasar and she asked to meet him. He became her mentor, friend and spiritual director. She became a Catholic and mystic. She experienced the passion of Jesus as did Clare and Angela of Foligno. Her insights from her ecstasies and spiritual journeys informed the theology of Von Balthasar.

She wished to form a community called the community of St. John, a secular institute. Von Balthasar made the painful decision to leave his beloved Jesuit order and for a while he was a persona non-grata, but after a while he found a bishop who incardinated him into his diocese. His collaboration with Adrienne continued and helped shape his work. Once again we have an example of two whose love consists in looking in the same direction together. They looked onto Jesus in love and hoped to draw others into that love. This is the key to Von Balthasar's work. Adrienne became increasingly weaker over the years and died in 1968.

Von Balthasar did a lot of work for the Church. Pope John Paul II asked him to become a cardinal in 1988. Von Balthasar tried to refuse but John Paul asked him to reconsider as a personal favour to him. Von Balthasar agreed but died suddenly, days before he would receive the red hat. Both men got their way.

The Mysteries of the Easter Season

Clare, Angela and Adrienne all entered into mystic union with Jesus in his agony, death and resurrection. Von Balthasar's genius lay in writing the insights of Adrienne and other mystics into his system. He was influenced as well by Soren Kierkegaard who saw our lives as being "contemporary" with the life of Jesus. Jesus' story wasn't a once and for all event in the past - his life and words are a drama in which we are involved. Von Balthasar saw the Holy Spirit as the Spirit of love who brought into a living relationship with the crucified and risen Jesus who is alive today. We are called to share with him in his work of salvation and healing of a fractured world.

For Von Balthasar "to say incarnation is to say Cross" (Mysterium Paschale, p.142). He says of Jesus the Christ "as God, and also as man, he exists only in relation to the Father in the unity of the Holy Spirit." (Der Antiromishe affekt, p.115). He says:

> The Son is Trinitarian revelation. He "produces on earth an extrapolation of the Trinity: he lives in a completely Trinitarian way, though he becomes a man among men"... "He lives in the Holy Spirit, whom he receives, and in the vision of the Father, with whom he speaks in prayer, and whose will He does." (TD 3, p.198).

The centre of theology for Hans Urs Von Balthasar and Adrienne Von Speyr is the obedience of the incarnate Son to the Father.

At the beginning of all his work there is found obedience: the readiness to let himself be disposed of by the Father according to his total will. This is a letting go, an indifference that never chooses this as opposed to that. Already the way from the bosom of the eternal Father to the womb of the temporal Mother is a path of obedience, the most difficult and consequential of ways, but one which is trod on mission from the Father: "See, I come to do your will" (Heb. 10:7).

(Threefold Garland, p.30).

The word obedience is problematic. Strictly speaking there is no obedience in the love relationship between Father, Son and Holy Spirit. Obedience comes from the Latin meaning "from hearing". What the Father wishes becomes the son's wish. God's will is that all people be saved (1Tim 2:4). Jesus is God's word made flesh (Jn 1:14) and in the words of N.T. Wright, "God condemned sin in the flesh of his son" (Paul and the Faithfulness of God, p.898). Jesus entered the world of sin and alienation and experienced the fullness of that world - our world.

Mary's role in the incarnation of the son of God is important. Her "yes" to God allowed the son of God enter into our world of space and time.

The full consent of the Mother was already required at the time of the Incarnation of the Son... this Yes of Mary had to be a consent of total faith, without limit, without any restriction. For at least three reasons: first, because God, in becoming incarnate in the Virgin, does not violate his creature; secondly, because this Mother had to be capable of introducing her Son into the plenitude of Israel's religion, into perfect Abrahamic faith; thirdly, because the Incarnation of the Word requires precisely a flesh which itself welcomes him perfectly; in other words, because the faith of this Mother had to encompass her whole person, body and soul, it had to be an incarnate faith.

(Au Coeur du Mystère rédempteur p.53f)

For Hans Urs Von Balthasar and Adrienne Von Speyr, Mary's yes is the fundamental attitude of all Christian faith and love. Hans Urs and Adrienne point us to the immaculate heart of Mary because there is found the secret of true prayer. Praising God in the Magnificat, contemplating Jesus and his words in her heart, prayerfully awaiting the Holy Spirit with the Apostles came from the heart full of love. To be Mary is to be prayer (*Christlich Mediteren*, 1984, p.60). Mary's yes continues as her son begins his ministry. She now conforms her will to his.

> Jesus does not anticipate in his mind the destiny that is come; he just lets himself be guided, day by day, by the Father. His Mother likewise does not anticipate anything of what is to come. One of the features of her faith (which is the fulfilment of Abraham's) is constantly to accept only what God decrees.
>
> (*Maria für heute* - p.16f).

Mary is called to follow Jesus into the dark, faith reduced to utter nakedness. Mary's way is the dark and humble way of faith (St. Thérèse of Lisieux). Pope John Paul II in *Redemptoris Mater* spoke of Mary for love of her son entering the dark night of his suffering (*Redemptoris Mater*, n.61).

Her consent at the incarnation continues as she sees her son led to the cross. In the Holy Spirit who filled her from her conception, Mary on Calvary gives her son back to the Father. In the letting it be done of God's will in the power of the Holy Spirit she teaches us the way of abandonment and prayer. Her insight is that in the face of the pain of Calvary where Jesus feels abandoned and dies a sad and lonely death the Spirit is at work. He is forming a new creation. He is the same Spirit of the Book of Genesis who hovered over the chaos (Gen. 1:1). He now hovers over the chaos of Calvary bringing a new order from the tragedy of Jesus' death and Mary's infinite sorrow.

> The more seriously Christians take this letting-it-happen-in-me for themselves and their whole life of following Jesus,

the more Marian is their baptismal faith. But because of that they are also linked with Mary's gesture of giving back her Son, from the beginning as far as the Cross, to the Father in the Holy Spirit. The Son has to do all the work that the Father wants him to do, and so into that work he fits Mary and all mankind. (TD 3, p.376ff).

Our share in Jesus' Journey

For Von Balthasar, to say 'Eucharist' is to say sacrifice. The supreme thanksgiving to the Father was given by the incarnate son who gave his all, body and soul to the Father in his death on Calvary. We receive the grace to offer ourselves by offering and eating the paschal meal, the Eucharist. Adrienne saw this clearly. St. Paul speaks of Christians "sharing the sufferings of Christ" (see Phil 3:10) by which he means that Christians, by the grace of Jesus, are able to offer their sufferings, in union with his, to the Father thereby cooperating in Jesus' work for his Church (cf Col 1:24). It is only in union with the sacrifice of the altar that we make this offering.

Von Balthasar speaks of Christian existence as "pro-existence. The incorporation of the faithful into the body and work of Christ has the consequence that they share in Jesus' work 'for us'" (Theodrama 3, p.379). Our lives are lived in union with Jesus. Paul uses the expression "in Christ". In union with him our prayer and works extend to others. The French writer Léon Bloy, said: "An act of love, the stirring of gentle compassion, sings the praises of God from Adam to the ends of the world, heals the sick, comforts the desperate, stills storms, frees prisoners, converts unbelievers, shields the whole human race." (Le Désepéré (Paris 1964), p.113). This is a commentary on the prayer of Clare, Angela and Adrienne.

Adrienne found herself in mystic communion with suffering humankind. During the war, though physically resident in neutral Switzerland, Adrienne plunged deep into the agonies of her fellow men and women.

We sat on the terrace above the Rhine. On the far bank is Germany. She feels the suffering, the world's anguish. At that very time the great Russian offensive begins. A million dead, the Russians say. She groans aloud. She hears clearly, in her own ears, the cries of death, the screaming of mothers, those who weep and give up their sons, and the even worse screams of those who do not give up their sons, who do not want to weep. In the river's roar and the faint hum of the city she hears the noise of the world. It seems peaceful, but in reality it is very different. In reality everything is screaming, every person, every creature. I hear the cries quite clearly. I can hardly bear it. Everywhere - deep down - is fear.

(Erde Und Himmel (1), p.93f).

Throughout her life Adrienne suffered terribly: in spirit with inner darkness and godforsakeness, in body with diabetes, heart trouble, near blindness and a lingering mortal illness. She offered it all up in union with Jesus by the power of the Holy Spirit to the Father in faith praying to ease in some way the pain of her fellow men and women. She says: "As soon as a person has inwardly said yes to some trial, to some suffering, it is used further afield and has an effect on other people." (Erde und Himmel (1) p.341). Adrienne's life, along with Clare and Angela, are living testimonies to this statement.

Going to the Cross: Good Friday (Mysterium Paschale, p.89-116).

The passion began in Gethsemane when Jesus falls to the ground (Mk 14:35). He feels the great testing and fears the 'peirasmos'. Everything starts from within: in fear 'ekthambeisthai' and the horror which isolates (Mk 14:33). He feels the abandonment of the Father. He prays 'dear Father', 'Abba', yet he hears no voice. He is the loneliest person in the universe.

Von Balthasar quotes St. Bonaventure (P.103ff). He produced a distinction between passion and compassion. His suffering is a co-suffering with broken humanity. He is in solidarity of love with all of broken humankind.

In terms of the pain of suffering, *passio*, Christ suffered more intensely in his sensitivity; in what concerns the pain of co-suffering, *compassio*, he suffered more intensely in his spiritual nature. The pain of co-suffering was greater than the pain of suffering.

Christ's excess of love made him more inclined to suffer. The stronger the love is, the more painful are the wounds of co-suffering.

And so his co-suffering goes beyond all other co-suffering, just as his suffering goes beyond all other (bodily) suffering, for the excess of his love transcends that of all suffering. His compassion embraces all people. He shows God's love of his people.

On the cross Jesus cries out "My God, my God, why have you forsaken me?" (Mk 15:34). In the end Jesus gave out a loud cry and breathed his last (Mk 15:37).

In Paul's letter to the Phillipians we read:

> "His state was divine,
> Yet he did not cling
> to his equality with God
> but emptied himself
> to assume the condition of a slave,
> and became as men are;
> and being as men are,
> he was humbler yet,
> even to accepting death,
> death on a cross" (Phil 3:6-8).

The Greek word for self-emptying is '*kenosis*' from the word '*kenoo*'. It shows the divine nature of Jesus that he gave himself away to experience the pain of godforsakenness, physical cruelty and infinite loneliness. The only person who could do this is a divine person:–

'By letting go of the 'form of God' that was his (and so his divine power of self-disposal) he willed to become the One who, in a remarkable and unique manner, is obedient to the Father - in a manner, namely, where his obedience presents the kenotic translation of the eternal love of the Son for the 'ever-greater' Father. To this extent, that 'inspiration' by the Father which we spoke of above is not simply the inner élan of his love, but submission to the rule and leading of the Holy Spirit of mission who 'impels' him (Luke 4, 1 and 14, etc.). In the time of the Son's abasement, the Spirit (proceeding eternally from Father and from Son) receives a primacy over the Son who obeys him (and by him obeys the Father): this constitutes the expression of the fact that all of his existence is ordered, functionally and kenotically, to the Cross. Even those great affirmations which begin with the word 'I' are not the language of 'self-consciousness' but of mission.'

(Mysterium Paschale, p.90f).

Yet the Father is present and the Holy Spirit is active. Jesus' agony is under the power of the Holy Spirit. His death is not the end. The Son in his total self-giving gives the love of God to the world. This love is glorified by the Father who raises Jesus from the dead (Glory of the Lord, I, p.535). Jesus loves to the end.

Holy Saturday:

The descent into Hell is part of the Christian tradition. For example the fourth general council of the Lateran (1215) says: "He descended into Hell, rose again from the dead, and ascended into Heaven." It is one of Adrienne's great contributions to show that Jesus' soul truly entered the world of Hell. In her mystic communion with Jesus she experienced the pain of loss that those without God feel. She felt the loneliness of Jesus. Jesus does not descend into Hell as rich but as dead. As Aquinas said between dying on Good Friday and being raised from the dead on Easter

Sunday, Our Lord is not a man but a dead man. In his soul the son of man experiences the powerlessness of every spirit in Sheol.

> Christ did not (as in the icons of the Eastern Church) descend as the victorious Risen One - Holy Saturday is not Easter - but as the Dead One, who no longer speaks as the Word of God, or rather "has become the silent Word of the Father". And so we have to learn to share this silence between Death and Resurrection.
>
> (Maria für heute, p.56).

The Divine Word enters the total speechlessness of death... He is now the silent "Word". He now shares our ultimate destiny - he is in solidarity with the dead.

> The ultimate consequence of the redemptive mission he has received from the Father is to be in solidarity with the dead, or rather to be in solidarity with that death which for the first time makes the dead really dead.
>
> (Mysterium Paschale, p.248).

As depicted in the Old Testament Sheol means helpless isolation, inactivity, remoteness from men and from God. This Sheol of the Old Testament is the Hell Jesus enters. Christ's very presence in this solitude is transforming and solidic when seen in conjunction with his resurrection and ascension. The descent into Hell is the final stage of the Son's paschal journey to the Father. In this Hell of infinite loneliness Jesus brings his love. He shows that God's love is offered to all. In this Sheol Jesus puts himself in the place of all sinners. He is in solidarity with the broken. He substitutes for the fallen. His grace and mercy are always faithful and always seeks out the fallen and broken. It is the genius of Clare, Angela and Adrienne to contemplate this divine mercy and allow it radiate from their lives.

Adrienne and Von Balthasar say that some souls in this life are given the grace of experiencing with Jesus his experience in Sheol, not as an end in itself, but that, in Christ and with Him by the power of the Holy Spirit, they can assist their brethren in the church. I think of those who find themselves plunged into the black hole of depression, abuse and rejection. Angela of Foligno experienced this dark night of loneliness and felt all the temptations of the past assail her. She was one with Jesus in his agony in Sheol.

We may be allowed into the Lord's Passion, even into his Hell, but this paradox is inescapable: I suffer with him, but he at the same time he suffers for me.

Easter Day and Afterwards

The Welsh poet, D. Gwenallt Jones says:

> He did not fling our bit of flesh like a rag on the rubbish-dump of Gehenna,
> Or throw our blood there like a bottle of worn-out medicine,
> But raised them from the grip of the worms' incomparable three days,
> A transparent spiritual body, the perfection of man and God.
> (see *Poetry of Wales*, ed. R. Gwenallt Jones (1974)
> p.112f).

Von Balthasar and Karl Barth agree on this point. The resurrection is objective and real: "The Lord has truly risen" (Lk 24:34). It is something that happened to the body of Jesus and could be perceived by the followers of Jesus, in their minds and in their hearts and by sight.

> The Resurrection is a Trinitarian event... it is the Father who, as "the God of the living" (Rom. 4:17) awakens the Son from among the dead so that he, as one freshly united with the Father, can send forth God's Spirit into the Church.
> (Mysterium Paschale, p.257 see also 269-281).

It is God the Father who takes initiative for the resurrection of the Son is the fulfillment of his creative work. He is always faithful. Jesus is a new creation. It is through the power of the Holy Spirit that the Father raises Jesus from the dead (cf Rom 8:11). The idea of a dead man coming back to life is strange. Yet in Jesus one who did so was seen and heard. Mary Magdalen and others experienced his presence. Jesus' death was a work of his love, a work that was one with the Spirit of love, the Holy Spirit. This love is involved in his return to life. "Love is strong as death." (Canticle of Canticles 8:6).

The sending of the Holy Spirit by the ascended Son completes the Easter mystery. Only after the Son has been glorified can the Paraclete be sent (John 7:39). Luke and John differ in their time scales for the pouring forth of the Spirit, yet this central point is that Jesus returns to the Father so that the Holy Spirit can be poured out on those who follow Jesus.

> The Spirit is not bestowed before the Triduum Paschale (Jn. 7:39). When this mission is "accomplished", Jesus "breathes out" his Spirit and gives him back to the Father (Lk. 23:46; cf. Mk. 15:37; Mt. 27:50; Jn. 19:30); then, when he is risen, as disposer of the Spirit, he breathes him into the Church (Jn. 20:22), the Spirit, both sevenfold and single, of suffering and of resurrection, who leads all who follow Jesus into a wholly new form of dramatic existence.
>
> (TD 3, P.341f).

Clare:

Clare contemplated these mysteries throughout her life. She experienced in her heart this infinite love of God. St. Francis sent troubled friars to her so she could heal them (FF 2958). He himself in his last illness entrusted himself to Clare and her sisters. In this light we understand Clare's words to Agnes of Prague:

> Place your mind before the mirror of eternity!
> Place your soul in the brilliance of glory!
> Place your heart in the figure of the divine substance
> and, through contemplation,

transform your entire being into the image
of the Godhead Itself,
so that you too may feel what friends feel
in tasting the hidden sweetness
that, from the beginning,
God Himself has reserved for His lovers.

And, after all who ensnare their blind lovers
in a deceitful and turbulent world
have been completely passed over,
may you totally love Him
Who gave Himself totally for your love,
At Whose beauty the sun and the moon marvel,
Whose rewards and their uniqueness and grandeur have no
limits;
I am speaking of Him,
the Son of the Most High,
Whom the Virgin brought to birth
and remained a virgin after His birth.

(3LAg in *The Lady*, p.51)

Chapter 4

The Cross: Love and Acceptance

For most people, the Franciscan tradition evokes images of joy not tears. In some instances tears are indeed a sign of joy. Bonaventure writes of Francis at the crib of Greccio: "The man of God stands before the crib, filled with affection, bathed in tears and overflowing with joy" (LM 10.7). When his father was pursuing him in anger, Francis begged for deliverance with a flood of tears that produced an experience of excessive joy (LM 2.2). One day, while weeping for his sins, Francis experienced the joy of the Holy Spirit's forgiveness (LM 3.6).

But the symbol of tears is linked above all with redemption. Bonaventure asks readers to weep for their sins and for others, to weep at the sufferings of Christ, indeed to join their tears to those of Christ. Again, Francis is the model. Bonaventure often recalls how Francis wept daily and so weakened his eyes by tears that he lost his sight (DM, 69, 122, 138; LM 5.8; 8.1). According to Thomas of Celano, Francis's first "official" biographer, Francis "wept bitterly because of the Passion of Christ, which he almost always had before his eyes. Remembering the wounds of Christ, he filled the roads with laments, without finding consolation." And after his experience before the crucifix at San Damiano, Francis had a "holy compassion for the Crucified" fixed in his soul (2Cel 10).

The sources also tell us that Clare's prayer was often suffused with tears. The author of *The Legend of Saint Clare* presents an image of Clare as another Mary Magdalene, weeping and kissing the feet of Jesus. The author confuses Mary Magdalene with Mary of Bethany. In her sleep, an angel of darkness comes to Clare to deter her from weeping, threatening that it will cause her to go blind or to dissolve her brain (Lg C 49). Clare wept when a sister was sad or tempted (Lg C 38), and when Clare wept at prayer, her tears moved other sisters to tears of sorrow as well (Proc 1.7; 3.7; 6.4; 10.3). Clare wept with the suffering Christ and even wept as she taught the novices to do the same (Lg C 30).

St. Clare lived a life of love and in her rule she called on her sisters to a life lived in love (e.g. see Reg C I, III, etc.). She knew the love of God revealed in Jesus Crucified and tried to inculcate that love in her life. In her letter to Erementude of Bruges she says: "Let us pray for one another for by carrying each other's burdens of charity in this way we may easily fulfill the law of Christ" (The Lady, p.421). The love of Clare was rooted in the love Jesus has for all people and that love was poured into her heart by the Holy Spirit.

The cross revealed the total love of Jesus for suffering humanity. Clare meditated and prayed before the cross and in it she saw the 'mirror' of love. She led others, including her novices, to follow this way of life and made the love of God revealed in Jesus the focus of their lives.

> Crying over the Lord's passion was well known to her. At times she poured out feelings of bitter myrrh at the sacred wounds. At times she imbibed sweeter joys. The tears of the suffering Christ made her quite inebriated and her memory continually pictured Him Whom love had profoundly impressed upon her heart. She taught the novices to weep over the Crucified Christ and, at the same time, what she taught with her words, she expressed with her deeds. For frequently when she would encourage them in private in such matters, a flow of tears would come before the passage of her words. During the Hours of the day, at *Sext* and *None*, she was usually afflicted with a greater sorrow as she was immolated with her immolated Lord.

> One time, in fact, while she was praying *None* in her little cell, the devil *struck her on the cheek*, filled her eye with blood and her cheek with a bruise. She repeated more frequently the *Prayer of the Five Wounds of the Lord* so that she might nourish her mind on the delights of the Crucified without any interruption. She learned the Office of the Cross as Francis, a lover of the Cross, had established it and recited it with similar affection. Underneath her habit she

girded her flesh with a small cord marked with thirteen knots, a secret reminder of the wounds of the Saviour.

(Lg C 30).

The tenth witness at the process of canonisation, Sister Agnes, the daughter of Oportulo de Bernardo of Assisi mentions the prayer to the five wounds of the Lord. She did so in the context of recounting Clare's instruction on prayer to the sisters. She recited for them the "Prayer of the Five Wounds of the Lord". In it she says: "Strengthen me in good works that I might love you with all my heart, all my soul, and all my strength..." (The Lady, p.424). Clare would bless the ill with the sign of the cross and many healings were reported.

Another boy from Perugia with a sickness that completely covered his eye was brought to the holy servant of God. Touching the eye of the boy, she made the sign of the Cross on it and said: "Take him to my mother so that she might repeat the sign of the Cross over him." Her mother, Lady Ortulana, as I have said, having followed her little plant, had entered the Order after her daughter and used to serve the Lord as a widow with the virgin *in the enclosed garden*. The eye of the body, after it had received the sign of the Cross from her, purified of its illness, saw clearly and distinctly. Clare, therefore, insisted that the boy had been healed by the merit of her mother; the mother turned the burden of praise towards her daughter and considered herself unworthy of such an event.   (Lg C 33).

Clare had wonderful devotion to the sacrament of the Eucharist. Here the saving events of Jesus' passion and death were made present in sacrament. "When receiving the Body of the Lord, however, she at first shed burning tears, and approaching with trembling she feared [him who was] hidden in the Sacrament is less than [Him who was] ruling heaven and earth' (Lg C, 28).

Paul the apostle spoke of the mystery of the cross. In his first letter to the Corinthians he recalls his experience when he first began to preach among them: "When I came to you, I did not come proclaiming to you the testimony of God in excellence of speech or wisdom. I did not think it appropriate to preach anything among you except Jesus Christ and him crucified." (1 Cor 2: 1-2). He expands on what he had said in the first letter when he spoke of Christ crucified, "to the Jews an obstacle that they cannot get over, to the pagans madness, but to those who have been called whether they are Jews or Greeks, a Christ who is the power and wisdom of God." (1 Cor 1:25). Paul gives his life to Christ. He says in the letter to the Galatians: "I have been crucified with Christ and I live now with my own life but with the life of Christ who lives in he. The life I now live in this body I live in faith: faith in the son of God who loved me and who sacrificed himself for me" (Gal. 2:20 f). By the power of the Holy Spirit he has become one with Christ. He looks on the one who suffered for him and sacrificed himself so that Paul may have life. The love of God was poured into his heart "by the Holy Spirit given him" (Rom 5:5). St. Clare's life was a living example of what St. Paul spoke of and experienced.

When St. Bonaventure wrote the "Journey of the Mind into God" he looks at the figure of St. Francis who received the wounds of Christ on his body. What strikes Bonaventure is what Francis has become in Christ and how his transformation in Christ transformed the world around him. He saw Francis as a sacrament of God in the world and saw in him one who was conformed to Christ who brought peace to many. He has become other-centred and found his truest self in relation to the other, an I-Thou relationship with Christ and then to the brothers and sisters for whom Jesus died.

The mystical relationship of the human person to God through the living love of the Crucified leads one to the heart of God. What Bonaventure illuminates in the Life of Francis is that God, present in the word, calls out to us from the cross. He calls out to us that we may find him, and in finding him, love him and in loving him, that we may love the world in him. As he writes in his soliloquy: "Christ on the cross bows his head, waiting for you, that he may kiss you... that he may embrace you... that he may enrich you... that he might give himself totally" (Soliloquy I, 39).

The Cross in Paul Tillich

Paul Tillich (1886-1965) was a remarkable and a singular theologian who was as much at home in a philosophical discussion as he was in the pulpit and seemed as keenly interested in art and politics as he was in his work as a professional theologian. His attacks on Nazism led to the banning of his books, his dismissal from Frankfurt University and, ultimately, to his departure for the United States in November 1933. He continued to live and work in America after the war, engaging in many lecture tours around the world. Tillich was influenced by the early Franciscan movement, especially St. Bonaventure.[1] He helps express their ideas in a modern way for us.

The cross, according to Tillich, is effective because it is the final revelation. As revelation, it is not merely the communication of knowledge, it is an event which changes the structure, meaning and aim of existence. When revelation on the Cross is called 'final', this does not mean that it is the last in a temporal sequence. The word 'final' here means definitive, ultimate and unsurpassable. A revelation can only have this quality when the medium, the bearer of revelation, exhausts himself in the revelatory act. He denies himself without losing himself.

Tillich explains this phrase by pointing out that, since every revelation is conditional by the medium in and through which it appears, our ultimate concern can only be present when the bearer of that revelation denies its own ultimacy. This he says can only happen in the personal life process of "one who is united with the ground of being and meaning without separation and disruption" (Systematic Theology, I, p.133) and who in the act of resigning all claims to ultimacy "becomes completely transparent to the mystery he reveals" (ibid). Final revelation is rather the answer to our most basic human need: the need to escape from our situation of estrangement, of alienation, of separation from others, of the

---

[1]See especially Ewert H. Cousins, *Bonaventure and the Coincidence of Opposites* (Chicago: Franciscan Herald Press, 1978); John Dourley, "God, Life and the Trinity in the Theologies of Paul Tillich and St. Bonaventure," in *S. Bonaventura 1274–1974* (Rome: Collegio S. Bonaventura Grottaferrata, 1974) 4:271-82.

meaningless of so much in life, of despair and of the nihilism of violence.

Only the presence of God in our midst, in an alienated world and with us in our alienation, can penetrate this darkness, can bring our estrangement to an end and give us the reconciliation, creativity and hope we need. And this is precisely what revelation is and does. It is the presence of God in our midst, in our brokenness. He is in our world and a part of it. This is the place of the Cross and it is only the power to transform human existence. Only the "final" or "ultimate" revelation can bring our estrangement to an end and the revelation is final when the one who bears it rejects all claim to ultimacy for himself and, in virtue of this, is entirely transparent to God. This is what happens on the Cross.

Tillich asserted that the Cross has the power to transform the structure, meaning and aim of human life, because it is the Cross that God himself participates without reserve in human existence. It is there that he participates in our estrangement, alienation, suffering and death. The human condition is one of separation and alienation from God: but he has brought that suffering and alienation to an end by entering into it, taking it upon himself and by making it his own.

Jesus speaks of the Father and involves him in all he does. On the Cross, God takes the estrangement, meaningless and the despair of human existence into himself and in him they are stripped of their destructive power. God allows the hate fate of suffering and death to overtake his Son, and the Son becomes vulnerable to the negativeness of life. God, the Father, is with Jesus when life turns against him. He is with him when he encounters the ultimate rejection of life, and as a result death will never be again a sign of the absence of God and of our separation from him. In entering this negativity Jesus experiences different Godforsakeness - yet this Godforsakeness is different because in this moment God is close to him, even though Jesus experiences the pain of Godforsakeness.

God is for him powerless and Tillich finds the manifestation of that power in God's atoning activity which must be described "as his participation in our estrangement and in its self-destructive uniqueness" (Systematic Theology, 2, p.171). God reunites us, not by pretending that we are not estranged or that we have not offered ourselves against him, but by being present to us when and where we exist. These aspects of our lives which separate us from God are transformed, Tillich uses the classical "Logos". He uses this "Logos" (Word) Christology to demonstrate the power of God's participation in our brokenness. The Logos, the divine principle of self-manifestation "reveals the mystery and reunites the estranged, by appearing as a historic reality in a personal life" (Systematic Theology 2:112). John in his Gospel uses the term 'Logos' which is translated as word - "the word was made flesh" (Jn 1:14).

Because God in Christ has taken his place in our midst, suffering remains but it is no longer a sign of our alienation from or of his absence from our world. He is present to us and for us. Once God, in his Son, has taken his place with us in the midst of pain and suffering, once he has participated in our estrangement in taking this upon himself (Systematic Theology 2:175), there will be no dark corner of our human existence which will mean separation from Him. We are accepted. We are loved.

Participation as Acceptance

Tillich affirms that God's participation in the negativity of existence is an act of acceptance and of love (Systematic Theology, 3:225). This acceptance is God's reconciling act which brings about a change in the human situation. The separation between God and human beings is overcome. Christ as the new being mediates the reconciling act of God to people. In Jesus the Christ God's acceptance of us has reached into our lives in their totality and has encountered us at the heights and depths of the human condition, because in him God has participated in the depth of human existence. (Systematic Theology, 1:270). God's existence is not some form of blind tolerance. On the Cross he forgives us and claims us. Real love consists in the sharing the condition and destiny of the other. On the cross he extends to us reconciliation.

Reconciliation is the absence of all barriers which separate God and human beings. Tillich uses the traditional term 'agape' to describe the kind of acceptance and love that comes to expression on the cross. 'Agape' has certain qualities that raises it above other forms of love and gives it the power to transform them. It is receptive because it accepts the one who is loved unconditionally and without restriction. It is paradoxical because it holds on to this acceptance in spite of the estranged and altered states of those who are loved. It is anticipatory because it shapes the restoration of holiness, the greatness and dignity of the beloved through the very act of accepting him or her.

The Cross is the expansion and realisation of this love. It is the source of the message "which is at the very heart of Christianity and makes possible the courage to affirm faith in the Christ; mainly that, in spite of all the forces of separation between God and men, this is overcome on the side of God." (The Dynamics of Faith, p.123). It is through the Cross that this loving acceptance can touch human life.

When St. Francis prayed before the Cross of San Damiano and saw the brokenness of crucified love, he came to know he was loved. He was enabled to accept his own brokenness and heart. He was firstly reconciled to himself. To truly love oneself is the grace of all graces. In being reconciled to himself he became reconciled to the "other" and loved others as God loved them. He developed a universal love and expression for all God's world. This is the Cross Clare would have seen every day in San Damiano when she and the Poor Clares took residence there.

Clare and Francis had special devotion to the Eucharist. To proclaim the death of the Lord is to accept the Eucharist as the same revelation as that of the Cross, and for this reason Eucharist is a call to understand our lives and ourselves in a new way. Eucharist is a call to us to accept what God has said of himself in Jesus - we are accepted and loved. Eucharist celebrates the fact that God has participated in the negativities of our lives and in so doing has created a domain of shared existence in which he has united himself and his destiny with ours. In doing this God has claimed us totally. We can be our weak and vulnerable selves because we can rejoice in the presence of the one "who calls into being the things that do not yet exist and raises the dead to life" (See Rom 4:17). God is with us in our weakness to heal us and transform us. He asks us to share in the death and resurrection of his son and live by the power of the Holy Spirit. We are people who have received a great gift and we give thanks - the precise meaning of the Greek word 'eucharistein'.

Accept that you are accepted

In his work "The Courage to Be" Tillich says that faith bridges the gap between us and the transcended God in the fact of accepting that we are accepted (p.172). It takes courage to do this - to offer being in the face of non-being as Tillich describes it (ibid.). It takes courage because of the many negativities of life that can make us think we are not loved or lovable. Yet God is the ground of our being and his nature is love (1 Jn 4:8,16). He loves us totally. Tillich once said that to fully appreciate his thought we should read his sermons.

One of his sermons is called "You are accepted" (in the 'Shaking of the Foundations', p.155-165). He asks who has not felt lonely in the midst of a social event? The feeling of our separation from the rest of life is most acute when we are surrounded by music and talk (p.158). We cannot penetrate the hidden centre of another individual nor can the individual pass beyond the shroud that covers us. Even the greatest love cannot break through the walls of the self. Who has not experienced that disillusionment of all great love? The state of our life is estrangement from others and ourselves, because we are estranged from the "Ground of our being", because we are estranged from the origin and aim of our lives. We are separated from the mystery, the depth and the greatness of our existence.

Tillich tells us that by the action of grace God enters our situation and by the power of the Holy Spirit, the author of grace teaches us we are accepted. In a beautiful piece he writes:

"We cannot transform our lives, unless we allow them to be transformed by that stroke of grace. It happens; or it does not happen. And certainly it does *not* happen if we try to force it upon ourselves, just as it shall not happen so long as we think, in our self-complacency, that we have no need of it. Grace strikes us when we are in great pain and restlessness. It strikes us when we walk through the dark valley of a meaningless and empty life. It strikes us when we feel that our separation is deeper than usual, because we have violated another life, a life which we loved, or from which we were estranged. It strikes us when our disgust for our own being, our indifference, our weakness, our hostility, and our lack of direction and composure have become intolerable to us. It strikes us when, year after year, the longed-for perfection of life does not appear, when the old compulsions reign within us as they have for decades, when despair destroys all joy and courage. Sometimes at that moment a wave of light breaks into our darkness, and it is as though a voice were saying: 'You are accepted. *You are accepted*, accepted by that which is greater than you, and the name of which you do not know. Do not ask for the name now; perhaps you will find it later. Do not try to do anything now; perhaps later you will do much. Do not seek for anything; do not perform anything; do not intend anything. *Simply accept the fact that you are accepted!*' If that happens to us, we experience grace. After such an experience we may not be better than before, and we may not believe more than before. But everything is transformed. In that moment, grace conquers sin, and reconciliation bridges the gulf of estrangement. And nothing is demanded of this experience, no religious or moral or intellectual presupposition, nothing but *acceptance*.   (p. 163 f).

Later on he says:

And in the light of this grace we perceive the power of grace in our relation to ourselves. We experience moments in which we accept ourselves, because we feel that we have been accepted by that which is greater than we. If only more such moments were given to us! For it is such moments that make us love our life, that make us accept ourselves, not in our goodness and self-complacency, but in our certainty of the eternal meaning of our life. We cannot force ourselves to accept ourselves. We cannot compel anyone to accept himself. But sometimes it happens that we receive the power to say 'yes' to ourselves, that peace enters into us and makes us whole, that self-hate and self-contempt disappear, and that our self is reunited with itself. Then we can say that grace has come upon us. (p. 164 f).

Chapter 5

Clare, a footprint of Our Lady
(see Leg C, Prologue)

May St. Paul in her book "Clothed with gladness" speaks of Mary and St. Clare. They lived a heart to heart relationship, a deeply personal I-Thou relationship. Together they reflected on the word of God. As Spirit-filled prayer and reflection change the person truly docile to their transforming power, so the Spirit-filled prayer of St. Clare led her into an identification with the Virgin Mary. She helped give birth to Christ in the souls who came to her. Those who follow in Mary's footsteps, by humility and in poverty, also carry Jesus in their hearts. They become one "in Jesus". She tells Agnes of Prague that if she does these things she will be "worthy to be called a sister, spouse and mother of the Son of the Most High Father and of the glorious Virgin" (1 L Ag 24). In the second letter she tells Agnes that she should become a second Rachel (2 L Ag 11). In medieval times Rachel was seen as a model of prayer, and contemplation. This goes back to St. Jerome (+419). He believed the name Rachel came from the Hebrew words ra'ah (to see) and halel (to begin). He interpreted this as one who saw the beginning.

In Chapter 6 of her Rule Clare quotes the "form of life" given to her by St. Francis. Francis speaks of "by divine inspiration you have made yourselves daughters and handmaids of the Most High, most Exalted King, the heavenly Father, and have taken the Holy Spirit as your spouse you have chosen to live according to the perfection of the Holy Gospel..." (Reg C, 6:3). This is the essence of living in a heart to heart relationship with Mary.

Clare goes on to quote St. Francis again:

> "I, little brother Francis, wish to follow the life and poverty of our most high Lord Jesus Christ and of His most holy Mother and to persevere in this until the end; and I ask you, my ladies, and I give you my advice that you live always in

this most holy life and poverty. And keep careful watch that you never depart from this by reason of the teaching or advice of anyone." (Reg C, 4:7).

Clare remained loyal all her life to this call of St. Francis and this showed itself as hoping for the "privilege of poverty".

Clare closed the first letter to Agnes of Prague by assuring her that she would pray for her in the innermost heart of Christ (1 L Ag 31). The medieval meaning of the term innermost heart (viscera) is the very centre of one's being, the seat of all affection and emotion. A stained glass window in the Basilica of San Francesco in Assisi illustrates Clare's image. On one side, the Christ child is held on the lap of his mother, Mary, who is standing. On the other side one sees St. Francis being held within the figure of the Christ. We and Francis are her children in Christ. Mary loves all her children. This shows the innermost heart of Mary which St. Clare loved and lived in communion with. When Angela of Foligno saw this image she fell into a swoon "...when I saw a stained glass window depicting St. Francis being clearly held by Christ, I heard him telling me: 'Thus I will hold you closely to me and much more closely than can be observed with the eyes of the body'" (Angela of Foligno Complete Works - New York, p.141-142).

At the process of Canonisation this tender loving of Clare inspired Sr. Cristiana to believe that the holiness of St. Clare was comparable to that of Mary, the Blessed Virgin (Proc 5:2). Sister Balvina, at the process said that only Mary could be regarded as holier than Clare. (Proc 7:11). All the witnesses told of Clare's kindness in community and her special care for the sick and vulnerable. The heart of Clare was a heart of love in the power of the Holy Spirit.

Francis de Sales and Jeanne de Chantal

Francis de Sales (1567-1622) was born in Château de Sales to the noble Jules family of the Duchy of Savoy. He studied in Paris. He had a conversion experience and healing in Paris which ultimately led to him becoming a priest, eventually becoming bishop of Geneva. He became noted for his deep faith and gentleness. He is noted for his gentle approach to all in the wake of the Protestant Reformation.

His great friend was Jeanne Francoise de Chantal (1572 - 1641). She married the Baron de Chantal when she was 20. The baron was accidentally killed in 1601. Chantal managed the estate and gave freely to needy neighbours. During Lent of 1604 she met Francis de Sales. They became close friends and de Sales became her spiritual director. Jeanne founded the Congregation of the Visitation with an outreach to the sick and poor.

Francis wrote "The Treatise on Divine Love" with the newly formed congregation founded by Jeanne in vision.

> "I must explain to you that we have in this city a community of young women and widows who have retired from the world so as to live together with one mind in God's service under the protection of his most holy Mother... Frequently I have tried to repay them by dispensing the holy word and I have delivered it to them both in public sermons and in spiritual conferences.... A large part of what I now share with you, I owe to this blessed community."
>
> (Treatise 1, preface, 48).

Friendship and direction and extended conferences all merge into the experience that was his. The general experimental content finds its significance in the experience that lies at the basis of Francis' life and of which his subsequent is both an explanation and expression. Francis was a young student at the Jesuit college of Clermont, reserved, diffident and unsure of himself and haunted by the fear that he was damned. This temptation comes to many people, as I can attest. They believe they have been rejected by God and when I meet those who come to me, I have to reassure them constantly until the moment of grace lifts their fears away. Francis' torment ended in the lovely chapel of St. Etienne-du-Gries. We know of this event from the account given at his process of canonisation by Jeanne:

"To give me strength to bear a difficulty of my own, he told me that when he was at college in Paris, he was tried by a state of extreme mental anguish firmly believing that he was doomed to go to hell and had no hope of salvation. This made him go cold with fear.... However terrible his state of mind, he held fast in the depth of his soul to his resolution to love and serve God with his whole strength while life lasted, and all the more lovingly and faithfully in this life as he thought he would have no chance of doing it in the next. This state of anguish lasted... about six weeks... and it was so violent that he could hardly eat or sleep and went thin and yellow as wax. One day, however, diving providence mercifully delivered him.... Coming to a certain church... he went in to say his prayers. He knelt down in front of an altar of our Lady where he found a little wooden board on which was mounted a copy of the prayer beginning: 'Remember, O most loving Virgin Mary, that no one ever turned to you and was left forsaken....' He said it right through, rose from his knees and at that very moment felt entirely healed; his troubles, so it seemed to him, had fallen about his feet like a leper's scales."
(St. Francis de Sales: A Testimony by St. Chantal 1967, p44-45).

Paul Tillich said that spirit filled prayer has a healing power on the human person (Eternal Now, 63, 115) because of the elevation of the centre of the personality to God (Systematic Theology 1:127). Health is the same as salvation and is a life lived in faith and love. Prayer is directed under the impact of the Spiritual Presence (Tillich's word for the presence of God in the Holy Spirit). Prayer engenders in the person the strength to accept oneself as accepted by God (Systematic Theology, 2:178-179), in short the Courage to be (The Courage to Be, 180-81). This is true healing. This leads to a life of devotion to God in the Spirit. Jesus is alive and by the power of the Holy Spirit he is present among us. Francis experienced this loving presence and it transformed his life.

Francis saw from this moment that God's will was that all be saved (cf 1 Tim 2:5). He saw the call of all human life to that charity which was friendship and salvation. "This redemption, abundant, superabundant, magnificent and excessive.... so that no men can complain as if God's mercy were lacking to anyone" (Treatise, II, 4,113). "Each of us has a different even an abundant measure of all things required for salvation." (Treatise, II, 7,120). When Francis in his time stated this position, he was not alone but he was most definitely in a minority.

Francis did not see a distinction between spirituality and theology. What he had learned through his trial marked his life. His spirituality and theology were one. To someone who experienced a similar trial to the one he had experienced he said: "My soul, which endured the like for six long weeks, is qualified to compassionate to those thus afflicted." Those weeks of trial taught him "to have compassion on the infirmities of others" (H. Brémond, A Literary History of Religious Thought in France, 1:69). Francis saw the human being as one in need of love, ultimately the love that comes from God. All of his books and conferences can be seen in that light.

The way to enter this love is what he called the way to a life of devotion. He wrote his "Introduction to the Devout Life" with this mind. Devotion means generosity and magnanimity in love - as grace filled ability so that one can love frequently and properly. To live a Christian life one must have love. It is by love that we fly to the heart of God (John of the Cross and Thérèse of Liseaux were of the same mind). He said "Charity and devotion differ no more from one another than does flame from fire. Charity is spiritual fire and when it bursts into flame it is called devotion" (Introduction, I, 1, 39-41). The "Treatise on the Love of God" was written for those who had advanced in charity. Here he introduces the way the soul advances "into the excellence of divine love" (Treatise 1, preface, 40).

St. Francis and his Vocation

St. Francis of Assisi had come to know in his heart the love of God poured into our souls by the Holy Spirit, given us (Rom 5:5). He was not sure at one stage how to express this love in his life. St. Bonaventure recounts the following story for us:

"Choosing, therefore, two of the brothers, he sent them to Brother Sylvester, who had seen the cross coming out from his mouth, and, at that time, spent his time in continuous prayer on the mountain above Assisi. He was to ask God to resolve his doubt over this matter, and to send him the answer in God's name. He also asked the holy virgin Clare to consult with the purest and simplest of the virgins living under her rule, and to pray herself with the other sisters in order to seek the Lord's will in his matter. Through a miraculous revelation of the Spirit, the venerable priest and the virgin dedicated to God came to the same conclusion: that it was the divine good will that the herald of Christ should preach." (LM 12:2).

He felt drawn both to a life of contemplation and a life of action. Clare was one who gave herself to a life of contemplation. Louis Lallemant (1578-1635) was one who faced the same problem as St. Francis (of Assisi). His story helps us grasp how Francis of Assisi mixed contemplation with action. After making his studies in the Society of Jesus, Lallemant entered the order in 1605. He spent his years in teaching many young men, including some who would die as martyrs. His health was poor and he died in Bourges in 1635. Those whom he instructed kept notes and from these we have access to his thought. Lallemant gives the centrality of place to the Holy Spirit. We have to be guided by the Holy Spirit to discover who we are. His work is contained in a work called "The Spiritual Doctrine of Louis Lallemant..." In this work he says "We have in our hearts a void which all creatures are not able to fill. It can only be filled by God, who is our source and our end. The possession of God fills the void and makes us happy. The privation of God leaves us in that void and this renders us wretched." (Doctrine 1.1). This love of God is poured into our hearts by the Holy Spirit (see Rom 5:5). He sees the human being as an emptiness for God. God offers himself in the Spirit to this emptiness. The goodness of God is the source of his love.

Lallemant says that our emptiness must lead us to a purity of heart. This allows God to enter our hearts by the power of the indwelling and directing Spirit (Doctrine, IV, 2.1). Lallemant shows how the soul is led by a gradual and progressive development into a life of union with God. From this perspective we see how contemplation is the heart of being a Christian. "Contemplation is an awareness and presence of God and of things divine which is simple, free, penetrating, certain and proceeds from love and tends to love." (Doctrine II, 4.5). This union with God leads to expression in works (Doctrine VII, 4.9). In Lallemant's time there was a debate about which was the most important, contemplation or action. Lallemant showed the need for both to go together. In the life of Francis of Assisi he achieved this position. Clare achieved the life of the contemplative heart that is at the heart of Franciscan life. In the life of the Spirit we all have different roles (see 1 Cor 12). At the heart of all states of life is love (1 Cor 13). We are parts of each other and responsible for each other. In the cases of Francis and Clare, Francis de Sales and Jeanne de Chantal spiritual friendship enabled them to become the people God called them to be.

To know Jesus and the power of his love

Clare is like another Mary. Mary lived a quiet life in Nazareth as Thérèse pointed out. Her life was one of gentle prayer and support. She stood by the cross of her son (Jn 19:25-27) and when the apostles awaited the Spirit she prayed gently with them (Acts 2:1-13). St. Bonaventure's work Lignum Vitae (The Tree of Life) is a meditation on Christ's life from his eternal generation by the Father, through his incarnation and birth, his whole life and misery, and his passion, resurrection and ascension and his eternal life in heaven. In two of the events especially, Christ's birth in Bethlehem and his suffering on the cross, we see Christ through the eyes of the one that loved him most – Mary.

In the account of Jesus' birth Bonaventure first summarises Luke 2:1-18, emphasising Francis' perception of poverty and humility. "He chose to be born from a home in a stable, to be wrapped in swaddling clothes, to be nourished by virginal milk and to lie in a manger between an ox and an ass." When the scene has been set he bids the reader enter the scene as an actor in the drama. In this way he reminds us of St. Francis and the living crib at Greccio.

In the same way with the passion he draws the reader into the event by having him identify with Mary, showing her feelings of compassion for the suffering saviour. Addressing himself to Mary, Bonaventure says:

> "This blessed and most holy flesh - which you so chastely conceived, so sweetly nourished and fed with your milk, which you so often held on your lap, and kissed with your lips - you actually gazed upon with your bodily eyes now torn by the blows of the scourges, now pierced by the points of the thorns, now struck by the reed, now beaten by hands and fists, now pierced by nails and fixed to the wood of the cross, and torn by its own weight as it hung there."
>
> (Lignum Vitae 28).

By this identifying with Mary we can share Christ's suffering and penetrate to the meaning of his redemptive death. This is what Clare lived in her union of love with Mary.

Chapter 6

Never-ending Song of Love

Sister Benvenuta of Perugia was the third companion of Saint Clare. She knew Clare when the family had to flee to Perugia. At the canonisation process she recounts the following:

> The said witness also said that a certain brother of the Order of Lesser Brothers, Stephen by name, was mentally ill. Saint Francis sent him to the monastery of San Damiano so Saint Clare would make the sign of the cross over him. After she had done this, the brother went to sleep a little bit in the place where the holy mother usually prayed. Upon waking, he ate a little and then departed cured. Asked who was present at this event, she replied the sisters of the monastery were, some (still) living, others dead. Asked if she had known that brother beforehand, how many days she had seen him ill, and how much time well, she replied she did not know all these things, because she was enclosed. Brother Stephen, once cured, went on his way.
>
> (Proc 2:15)

This is Regius Armstrong's translation in '*The Lady*' (p.153). Some of the older translations I read used the term insanity instead of mental illness. I remember when I suffered from depression, I asked a friend of mine who was a psychiatrist was there any cure for depression. He said: "Love". I wondered in my heart of hearts if such a thing existed. The world I had found was cruel and cold - callousness running wild. This is why I was drawn to this incident in the life of Clare and Francis. It demonstrates the trust Francis had in the healing prayers of St. Clare. Br. Stephen was obviously tormented. It was only because he was greeted with love that he could trust St. Clare. A modern day mystic, Caryll Houselander (+1954) suffered from depression but she experienced healing from a vision of Jesus who she saw was in communion with suffering humanity. A psychiatrist friend asked her to visit some of her patients who were mentally afflicted. She loved them back to life. (As a young woman she had fallen in love with Sidney Riley, a spy, who influenced Ian Flemings's formation of the character James Bond).

Caryll's story helps us see what Clare did. She made Stephen welcome and gained his trust. This is not easy for the "mentally afflicted". She led to rest at her place of prayer. Sleep for the tormented soul is a great release. While he slept she prayed with all the love in her heart. This loving prayer brought solace to the tormented Stephen and he felt at ease. Love was at the heart of Clare's prayer. She loved Stephen back to life. We can gain an insight into this love when we read of Clare's use of the "Song of Songs" in her writings.

The Song of Songs of St. Clare[1]

We read in chapter 8 of the Canticle:

> "Ah why are you not my brother,
> nursed at my mother's breast!" (8:1).

We hear when Clare describes herself as the spouse who is also the sister of Our Lord Jesus Christ (1 LAg 12). There are also echoes of Mt 12:50 here. Clare is caught up in wonder in how God is made visible in human flesh:

> "O God-centred poverty,
> when the Lord Jesus Christ
> who ruled and still rules heaven and earth,
> who spoke and things were made,
> came down to embrace before all else" (1 LAg, 17).

The term "embrace" is a term of endearment. She goes on to say "If so great and good a Lord, then, on coming into the Virgin's womb, wanted to offer despised, needy and poor in this world, so that people who were poor and needy, suffering excessive hunger of heavenly nourishment,

[1]Chiara Giovanna Cremaschi, Il Cantico dei Cantici in Chiara d'Assisi, VM 75 (2004), 39-51.

may become rich in him, by possessing the kingdom of heaven, be very joyful and glad, filled with a remarkable happiness and a special joy" (1 LAg 19-21). She uses the language of being a pure, mother and daughter (1 LAg 12) to explain the love relationship that ought to exist between Agnes and Jesus. He enters with love into our darkness to bring light and healing. In this way we came to understand the healing of Stephen (see above).

In the third letter to Agnes she speaks in more poetic terms of Jesus, the divine lover.

> And, after all who ensnare their blind lovers
> in a deceitful and turbulent world
> have been completely passed over,
> may you totally love Him
> Who gave Himself totally for your love,
> At Whose beauty the sun and the moon marvel,
> Whose rewards and their uniqueness and grandeur have no limits;
> I am speaking of Him,
> the Son of the Most High,
> Whom the Virgin brought to birth
> and remained a virgin after His Birth.
>
> (1 LAg 15-17).

She goes on to describe how Mary carried Jesus in her womb, so we too are called to be like Mary giving birth to Christ in our souls.

> May you cling to His most sweet mother who gave birth to a Son Whom the heavens could not contain, and yet she carried Him in the little cloister of her holy womb and held Him on her virginal lap. Who would not dread the treacheries of the enemy of humanity who, through the arrogance of momentary and deceptive glories, attempts to reduce to nothing that which is greater than heaven itself? Indeed, it is now clear that the soul of a faithful person, the most worthy of all creatures because of the grace of God, is

greater than heaven itself, since the heavens and the rest of creation cannot contain their Creator; only a faithful soul is His dwelling place and throne, and this only through the charity that the wicked lack. The Truth says: Whoever loves me will be loved by My Father, and I too shall love him, and We shall come to him and make Our dwelling place with him. As the glorious virgin of virgins carried (Him) materially, so you, too, by following in her footprints, especially (those) of humility and poverty, can, without any doubt, always carry Him spiritually in your chaste and virginal body, holding Him by Whom you and all things are held together possessing that which, in comparison with the other transitory possessions of this world you will possess more securely.

(1 LAg 15-27).

Clare also sings a nuptial hymn in honour of her beloved in the same way as the bride speaks of the bridegroom in the "Song of Songs".

> Happy, indeed, is she
> to whom it is given to drink at this sacred banquet
> so that she might cling with her whole heart
> to Him
> Whose beauty all the blessed hosts of heaven
> unceasingly admire,
> Whose tenderness touches,
> Whose contemplation refreshes,
> Whose kindness overflows,
> Whose delight overwhelms,
> Whose remembrance delightfully dawns,
> Whose fragrance brings the dead to life again,
> Whose glorious vision will bring happiness
> to all the citizens of the heavenly Jerusalem,
> which (vision),
> since He is the radiance of eternal glory
> is the brightness of eternal light and
> the mirror without blemish.

Gaze upon that mirror each day,
O Queen and Spouse of Jesus Christ,
and continually study your face in it,
that you may adorn yourself completely,
within and without,
covered and arrayed in needlework
and similarly adorned
with the flowers and garments of all the virtues,
as is becoming, the daughter and dearest bride
of the Most High King.

(4 LAg 9-17).

The language used by Clare in the letters is the language of the love songs of the 'Canticle of Canticles' ('The Song of Songs'). The language of being spouse, embracing, the enclosed garden and the praises of the beloved were part and parcel of how the mystics spoke of the love of God in Jesus. Clare shows herself to be part of that line. It is only by using the language of love of the Canticle that Clare can speak of God who is love. In the canticle itself we read "I am my beloved's and my beloved is mine" (Canticle 6:3). There is a union of love between the bride and bridegroom and this is the language Clare uses to show the level of love with her beloved Jesus. The crucified one is the bridegroom for Clare. In his broken figure Clare sees the radiance of true love who gave himself so that we could have life (see 4 LAg 23). She sees the crucified one in all her brothers and sisters and in embracing Jesus she embraces them - we see one example among many in the case of Stephen. Clare exhorts Agnes "may you totally love him who gave himself totally for your love" (3 LAg 15). In Clare's final blessing to her sisters she says: "Always be lovers of your soul and those of all your sisters" (The Blessing, 14). This is a hidden gem in Clare's writings. She teaches her sisters about an appropriate self-love - a love that is born because we are the children of God and Jesus suffered and died for us that we might have life. In Mt 19:19 we hear Jesus say "Love your neighbour as yourself." We are loved and are called to love as we are loved. In Is. 43 we read God tells his people not to fear "because you are precious in my eyes, because you are honoured and I love you" (Is. 43:4).

When Clare tells Agnes to contemplate the mirror (4 LAg 15) she means that the mirror is a person, the person of Jesus (Cremaschi, p.44). His love transforms us and we become the person Agnes is called to be. The same is true for us. In Christ we become the people we are called to be (see TD3). The hardest thing for all of us is to accept we are accepted (Tillich) yet in Christ we see we are eternally loved. God is love (1 Jn. 4:6, 16) and he loves totally. This is the great event that Clare enters to. She calls Agnes (and through her us) to allow that love come into our hearts. She tells Agnes in the first letter: "Thus you took a spouse of a more noble stock, who will ever keep your virginity ever unspoiled and unsullied, the Lord Jesus Christ."

> "When in loving, you are chaste;
> In poverty, you become more pure,
> in embracing you are a virgin
> Where strength is more robust,
> generosity more lofty,
> Where difference is more handsome,
> love more courteous,
> and every kindness more refined,
> Where embrace always holds you."
>
> (1 LAg 7-10).

The bride is transformed by the love of the bridegroom. In the fourth letter she quotes the Canticle (1:3), she tells Agnes as she contemplates love that she may act:

> "Draw me after you
> Let us run in the fragrance of your perfumes,
> O heavenly Spouse"
>
> (4 LAg 30).

The Canticle of Canticles:

In Hebrew the title is "Shir Hashirim". This means that the song is the greatest of all songs. In English we translate 'shir hashirim' with either 'The Canticle of Canticles' or 'the Song of Songs'. Rabbi Akiba (+135

A.D.) said, "All the world is not worth the day that the Song of Songs was given to Israel; all the writings (Kethubim) are holy but the Song of Songs is the holy of holies" (Mishna Yadim, 3:5). Modern critical scholarship regards the book as a collection of erotic love poetry that celebrates the passion between a man and a woman. From the early centuries of Christianity the allegorical method took over. An allegory is where one thing is said but another is alluded to (see Ravasi, Il Cantico dei Cantici, p.128-132). The passionate love of God for his people is infinitely greater than the love of a man and woman. In this way the Canticle both has a literal meaning and can be interpreted allegorically. In the Old Testament itself we see the use of allegory in the prophetic writings. In Hosea and Ezechiel the relationship between a man and a woman is used to symbolise the love God has for his people of the covenant (Hosea 1-3; Ez. 16).

The Canticle itself recalls some of the themes of the book of Genesis. God made man and woman in his likeness (Gen. 1:28f) and sexual love between a man and a woman is holy. In Paradise when God created the world by the power of his word he saw it was good (Tôb (see Ct 1:2; cf Gen. 1:4, 10, 12, 18, 21, 25, 31). Desire (tesuga) in the garden is pure but after the fall became a source of suffering and abuse (Gen. 3:16). In the Canticle there is no domination by one partner over the other. The bond between them is love and there leads both the bride and the bridegroom to honour the other. The Canticle moves from the experience of intense longing to that of blissful enjoyment and then to longing once more. The woman seeks her absent lover and finds him. The alternation between presence and absence, exhilaration and dejection characterises the ebb and flow of love.
The part I want to look at now is 8:6f. It reads:

> Set me like a seal on your heart
> like a seal on your arm.
> For love is strong as death,
> jealousy relentless as Sheol,
> The flash of it is a flash of fire,
> A flame of Yahweh himself.
> Love no flood can quench,
> no torrents drown. (8:6-7).

These lines are spoken by the woman. the image of the seal conveys her desire for his constant presence. She compares the power of love to that of death and Sheol. For the Hebrews, these were often personified as unrelenting powers since no-one can escape them. True love ('ahábá) and adoration (qin'á) will prevail. qin'á here means ardour more than jealousy. The fiery quality of love is said to be 'a flame of Yahweh' (Shallebegyá), a flame that burns brightly (like the heart of Clare). The verse can mean that human love is a share in the divine love itself. No flood can quench this love. This refers to the powers of the sea and the Abyss (Is. 43:2; 51:10). The metaphor has shifted from fire to water but the point is still the same and refers to the power of love. In the New Testament the love of God is recalled in Jesus the Christ. Paul tells us:

> He not only died for us - he rose from the dead, and there at God's right hand he stands and pleads for us.
> Nothing therefore can come between us and the love of Christ, even if we are troubled or worried, or being persecuted, or lacking food or clothes, or being threatened or even attacked. As scripture promised: For your sake we are being massacred daily, and reckoned as sheep for the slaughter. These are the trials through which we triumph, by the power of him who loved us.
> For I am certain of this: neither death nor life, no angel, no prince, nothing that exists, nothing still to come, not any power, or height or depth, nor any created thing, can ever come between us and the love of God made visible in Christ Jesus our Lord. (Rom. 8:34-39).

Thérèse of Lisieux and the Canticle[2]

Throughout the Christian centuries a large number of saints and thinkers interpreted the Song of Songs as allegorical only. There was Origen

---

[2]For this section see Thérèse of Lisieux Story of a Soul, tras. John Clarke, Washington, 1976. Also R. Murphy, The Song of Songs and St. Thérèse, Carmelite Studies 5, 1990, 1-9. See J. O'Brien, O.F.M., Thérèse and the Little Way of Love and Healing, Athlone, 2013.

(+254) in the third century. Bernard of Clairvaux (+1153) wrote extensively on the Song of Songs. The famous Carmelites John of the Cross (+1591) and Teresa of Avila (+1582) used the Canticle for their meditation. Clare finds herself in the long line of great mystics. John of the Cross said that contemplation is a secret, peaceful and loving infusion of love, which if admitted will set the soul on fire with the Spirit of love. We see this in the case of Clare. For me a modern counterpart of Clare is the French Carmelite Thérèse of Lisieux (+1897).

Her autobiography contains quotations from the Canticle of Canticles and John of the Cross. Thérèse once said, "If I had the time I would like to comment on the Canticle of Canticles, in the book I have discovered such profound things about the union of the soul with the beloved" (see Murphy, p.7). Thérèse often quoted from Canticle 1:4 (in the Vulgate rendering), "Draw me - we will run" to refer to God's love drawing us to follow him.

Thérèse's extended comments of 1:4 appear in the final pages of her story, not long after she speaks of her vocation as "love". Having long decided to do heroic deeds for Christ, she finds after reading Paul's first letter to the Corinthians (1 Cor. 12-13). "MY VOCATION IS LOVE! Yes, I have found my place in the Church. In the heart of the Church, my Mother, I shall be love" (MsB, 3v). Her commentary on 1:4 is a commentary on this vocation. She is drawn by God's love and now, she as love draws others to God. Thérèse came to know the Song of Songs through the Divine Office and 'lectio divina'. 'Lectio Divina' means reading the text in a contemplative manner. Her interpretation of the Song is influenced by her life's experiences. When she spoke of her first Holy Communion she says: "Ah! How sweet was that first kiss of Jesus. It was a kiss of love. For a long time now Jesus and poor little Thérèse had looked at and understood each other. That day it was no longer a look; it was a fusion; they were no longer two" (MsA, 35r°). Thérèse understood the sacraments as a source of her life with God. Thérèse tells us it was one morning after her thinking after communion she came to understand the words of Cant. 1:4 (MsC 34r°). She says:

He made me (34r°) understand these words of the Canticle of Canticles: "DRAW ME, WE SHALL RUN after you in the odour of your ointments." O Jesus, it is not even necessary to say: "When drawing me, draw the souls whom I love!" This simple statement: "Draw me" suffices; I understand, Lord, that when a soul allows herself to be captivated by the odour of your ointments, she cannot run alone, all the souls whom she loves follow in her train; this is done without constraint, without effort, it is a natural consequence of her attraction for You. Just as a torrent, throwing itself with impetuosity into the ocean, drags after it everything it encounters in its passage, in the same way, O Jesus, the soul who plunges into the shoreless ocean of Your Love, draws with her all the treasures she possesses. Lord, You know it, I have no other treasures than the souls it has pleased You to unite to mine; it is You who entrusted these treasures to me, and so I dare to borrow the words You addressed to the heavenly Father, the last night which saw You on our earth as a traveler and a mortal. Jesus, I do not know when my exile will be ended; more than one night will still see me singing Your Mercies in this exile, but for me will finally come the last night.

There Thérèse interprets the "draw me" of the passage as a prayer asking Jesus to unite soul to hers, for he has won her heart. She uses an analogy: "If fire and iron had the use of reason and if the latter said to the other: 'Draw me' would it not prove that it desires to be identified with the fire in such a way that the fire penetrate it and drink it up with its burning substance and seem to become one with it" (MsC 35r° - 36v°). This, she adds, is her prayer: that Jesus draw her "into the flames of his love" and "unite (her) so closely that He live and act in (her)" (MsC 36r°). She put words on her experience and this helps us understand Clare. She and Thérèse were drawn by Jesus into the flames of his love. In 4 LAg 30 Clare said:

"Draw me after you
let us run in the fragrance of your perfume
O Heavenly Spouse"   (4 LAg 30).

Jesus' Healing

Jesus said: "Come to me all you who labour and are overburdened and I will give you rest. Shoulder my yoke and learn from me, for I am gentle and humble in heart, and you will find rest for your souls. Yes my yoke is easy and my burden light" (Mt 11:28f). We learn here that it is following Christ that we come to peace, because he is with us (Mt 28:28). In Hebrews 4:1-13 we hear of those who have entered into rest ("we who have believed have entered into that rest"). The presence of the kingdom means one finds repose in God. Jesus asks us to 'shoulder the yoke'. Yoke came to mean obedience and Jewish teachers spoke of the yoke of the Torah. For Judaism Torah is all that God has made known of his nature, character and purpose, and of what he wants of humans in being and doing (Moore 1, Judaism in the First Three Centuries, p.263). It is the full revelation of God and his will for men. So here Jesus is saying that he is the full revelation of God. In 11:27 Jesus had said that he knows the Father and is the full revelation of God. The disciples knew Jesus and learn from him. Our true peace is with God and our hearts are restless until they rest in him. (Augustine Confessions 1:1). Rest is related to the Hebrew word 'shalom'. This is the peace that comes when we enter a right relationship with God. Love for God and neighbour means the yoke will be easier. Jesus brings us into fellowship with him and by the power of the Holy Spirit walks with us (see TDNT, 6, p.45-51). He is gentle (*praus*) and we need not fear him. Like the divine wisdom (Sin 51:23-30), and like God in addressing Moses (Ex 33:14) Jesus offers "rest", which is not our ease (cf 17-39) but is a synonym for salvation, associated with the kingdom of God and eternal life. (When brother Stephen was brought to Clare as we saw at the start of the chapter (see Proc 2:15) he was in great mental distress, Clare welcomed him and reassured him, then she prayed and he discovered the "rest" of which Jesus spoke – he found healing in the love of God revealed in Jesus and in Jesus he found peace.

That leaves us with one question: How can we enter that "rest" of which Jesus spoke? However there are many times when illness, distress, shame or grief seem to us to be the ultimate reality. We become aware we feel far from God.

The Book of Genesis contains stories of creation and the fall. In Gen. 1:26 we hear God say: "Let us make man, in our likeness and image..." and then in 1:28 we read: "God created man in his own image, in the image of God he created them, male and female he created them." It is male and female together that is the image of God. We have a model here for how Francis and Clare together reflected God to a broken world. Their friendship and gentle union in prayer allowed the image of God be found in them and this radiated to others. The idea of image means that the pattern on which human beings are fashioned is to be sought outside the sphere of the created. (Gerhard Von Rad, Old Testament Theology, 1:145). Clare and Francis point out to us that we are loved by God. The "image" is the perfect mirror of God but in us the mirror is broken and out of focus. Jesus is the word of God made flesh (Jn 1:14) and he is the perfect "mirror" of God who is love (1 Jn. 4:8, 16). Gregory Palamas (+1359) from the Eastern Church teaches us about the value of silence. For him the monk does not pursue anything more than what every believer living in the world ought to pursue. What sets the contemplative nun or monk apart from the ordinary person is that they live removed from the normal hustle and bustle of life, and become the models of the spiritual life to those believers who do not live in monasteries or convents. Gregory spent a large part of his life as a monk in silence. John Damasene said in the eighth century that "Silence (Hesychia) gives birth to prayer, and prayer is the mantle of the vision of God". The aim of this silence is to achieve a state in which we can hear the voice of God. In the silence we discover obsessions, compulsions or addictions. We discover hearts that never seem to heal. We do not know the exact nature of Stephen's mental illness. Francis sent him to Clare. She is a model of the silent prayer we have been talking of. She welcomed him and radiated acceptance. Then she prayed gently once Stephen was at rest and when he was quiet the love of God was poured into his heart by the Holy Spirit (see Rom. 5:5). In this he found healing. He experienced the love that heals. Clare and Francis continue to inspire us to enter that peace (shalom) of a right relationship with God.

Chapter 7

Do Not Extinguish the Spirit

St. Francis and St. Clare speak of not extinguishing the spirit of prayer (FLCL 7. and RB6). They were both people of the Spirit. However, the Holy Spirit is for many the hardest to understand. Sue Gerhardt wrote a work called *"The Selfish Society"* (2010). She described our culture as a culture of selfish individualism, which has identified our material well-being with happiness. The world of the Spirit is ignored and despised. The poverty of Francis and Clare is the direct opposite of our society.

St. John tells us:

> "The wind blows wherever it pleases,
> you hear its sounds,
> but you cannot tell where it comes from or where it is going.
> This is how it is with all born of the Spirit."

> (Jn. 3:8)

This describes how we cannot tie down the Spirit to neat formulae. He is beyond category. Yet is is the Spirit who is the Spirit of life and love. He is ever creative and is the source of all creativity and of all life. Francis and Clare left selfishness behind to enter the world of the Holy Spirit - God's empowering presence in life. As the Spirit is referred to wind in Jn. 3:8, so we can feel ourselves moved to pray like birds of the air driven by the breeze. The Hebrew word 'ruach' could mean breath or wind and John taps into this tradition. Prayer can be described as the way we come to God. The Holy Spirit vivifies all the methods. As we grow in union with Christ and turn towards the Father, we do so in the power of Holy Spirit. We cannot tell where the wind comes or where it goes but we still can see people of the Spirit. These people become icons of the Spirit. Jesus is the supreme and perfect icon of the Spirit (see Heb. 1:1-4). The others became icons of the Spirit "in Christ".

St. Seraphim of Sarov (+1833)

Seraphim is one of the icons of the Holy Spirit. The Spirit is not seen himself but is seen in the people who give themselves to him. St. Seraphim is one such icon and his words and life throw light on Francis and Clare. He was born on the 19th July 1754. He was baptised with name Prochor. His parents Isidore and Agatha lived in Kursk in Russia. His family were merchants. During Prochor's youth he received healing and saw visions of Our Lady. In 1775 he visited Saint Dorothea in Kiev. She spoke of his vocation to him. In 1777 he entered the monastery of Sarov as a novice and here he was given the monastic name of Seraphim. He once again suffered a serious illness but once again he was cured when Our Lady appeared to him. Later Seraphim went out into the forest and lived an ascetic life, and penance. One time he was attacked and beaten up by two men. He refused to defend himself - he actually had an axe in his hand but threw it away. He was very critically ill after the attack but once again he received a miraculous healing. He refused to press charges against the man and in the face of mercy and goodness they repented. He returned to live in the monastery.

In 1815 he was told in a vision it was time to open himself to people. He opened the door of his cell and welcomed people. Thousands came to him and were cured. He brought solace to those in distress. He welcomed all with compassionate love. One time he was away from the monastery. The people who came to see him told their children to go ahead and see could they find Seraphim. When he saw the children he came out to meet them. "He is a child like us!" said one of the children. He was a man of deep love and compassion.

Seraphim died in 1833 praying before an icon of Our Lady. There are ample more things that could be put into any account of Seraphim's life, but even a passing reference to Seraphim's life shows us that Seraphim was a man of the Spirit. In his retreat in the forest he left spaces where he could commemorate the events in the life of Jesus. He travelled with him in prayer through Gethsemane, to Golgotha and finally to the resurrection and Pentecost. He once spent 1000 days in silence standing on a rock. He was a witness to the resurrection and lived in the Spirit of

God that was poured out at Pentecost. In his compassion and love and the charisms he received, he was an icon of the Spirit. He showed us the result of God's penance in our lives by the power of the Holy Spirit. In John's Gospel we hear Jesus say:

> "If anyone loves me he will keep my word,
> and my Father will love him,
> and we shall come to him
> and make our home with him." (Jn. 14:23).

At the centre of our being, the 'heart' in Biblical terms, dwells the tri-une God but too often the path to our true selves is blocked. We become afraid of the silence. Seraphim is one who went ahead of us to show us the way is possible by the power of God's Holy Spirit, the Lord and giver of life.

Nicolas Motovilov was one person Seraphim cured. He became a friend and disciple of Seraphim. The "Conversation with Motovilov" or "Conversation on the Holy Spirit" constitutes an important witness to Seraphim's holiness. In 1831 Seraphim and Motovilov spoke. Seraphim by an inspiration of the Holy Spirit knew that Motovilov had a question that was burning within him. He wanted to know what is the aim of the Christian life. Seraphim said: "Prayer, fasting, works of mercy - all this is very good but it represents only the means, not the end of the Christian life. The true end is the acquisition of the Holy Spirit." Motovilov was confused by Seraphim's answer.

> 'Father, you keep on saying that the grace of the Holy Spirit is the goal of the Christian life, but how or where can I see such a grace? Good works are visible, but can the Holy Spirit be seen? How can I know whether or not he is in me?...
> 'God-loving one,' replied Seraphim, 'I've already told you that it's very easy.... What more do you want?'
> 'How I long to understand completely!'
> Then Father Seraphim gripped me firmly by the shoulders and said,

'My friend, both of us, at this moment are in the Holy Spirit, you and I. Why won't you look at me?'

'I can't look at you, Father, because the light flashing from your eyes and face is brighter than the sun and I'm dazzled!'

'Don't be afraid, God-loving one, you yourself are shining just like I am; you too are now in the fulness of the grace of the Holy Spirit, otherwise you wouldn't be able to see me as you do.'

And leaning towards me Father Seraphim said quietly:

'Thank the Lord for this ineffable goodness: you may have noticed that I did not even make the sign of the cross; only in my heart I said this prayer to the Lord: "Lord, grant him the grace of seeing clearly, with the eyes of the flesh, that outpouring of your Spirit which you vouchsafe to your servants when you condescend to reveal yourself to them in the reflection of your glory." My friend, the Lord granted it instantly - merely at poor Seraphim's prayer... So, my friend, why not look at me?'...

Then I looked at the *starets* and was panic-stricken. Picture, in the sun's orb, in the most dazzling brightness of its noonday shining, the face of the man who is talking to you. You see his lips moving, the expression in his eyes, you hear his voice, you feel his arms round your shoulders, and yet you see neither his arms nor his body, nor his face, you lose all sense of yourself; you can see only the blinding light which spreads everywhere, lighting up the layer of snow covering the glade, and igniting the flakes that are falling on us both like white powder.

(see Donald Nicholl *Triumphs of the Spirit in Russia* p.51f).

Motovilov goes on to describe how he felt peace. The peace he felt in the Biblical 'Shalom'. 'Shalom' results from a relationship with God in love.

St. Francis wrote in his first admonition:

The Lord Jesus says to his disciples: I am the way, the truth and the life; no one comes to the Father except through me.

If you knew me, you would also know my Father; and from now on, you do know him and have seen him. Philip says to him: Lord, show us the Father and it will be enough for us. Jesus says to him: Have I been with you for so long a time and you have not known me? Philip, whoever sees me sees my Father as well.

The Father dwells in inaccessible light, and God is spirit, and no one has ever seen God. Therefore He cannot be seen except in the Spirit because it is the Spirit that gives life; the flesh has nothing to offer. But because He is equal to the Father, the Son is not seen by anyone other than the Father or other than the Holy Spirit.

(see *The Founder*, p.128).

But the son is revealed - the person of Jesus - he is the Word made flesh (Jn. 1:14). He is conceived by the power of the Holy Spirit and is made known to us by the Spirit.

Francis and Clare

St. Seraphim said that if one person found peace, then a thousand were saved. Francis and Clare achieved this contemplative peace. St. Seraphim why so many were drawn to them. Peace comes from an intimate I-Thou relationship with God. The Holy Spirit leads us into this peace (shalom). Here the Spirit doesn't work as if by magic. He enters our human situation and works from there. Clare's mother Ortoluna was very loving. This is what she passed on to Clare. Later in life she joined Clare's community in San Damiano. When Clare sought a way to give herself to God, she met Francis and through him left all. A deep friendship grew between the two - to use an expression from Zefferelli's film they became "Brother Sun and Sister Moon". The film has always caused controversy - but in the end Zefferelli's Francis is one who takes Jesus' words seriously. "You cannot serve both God and wealth." (Mt. 6:24). The story as shown by Zefferelli in his film of Francis and Clare is not historical but it does catch something of the true affection that dwelt between them.

The friendship of Francis and Clare is where the Holy Spirit worked to bring both Francis and Clare to peace. They became beacons of light for the poor and broken. The generation they belonged to was one where courtly love was much praised and talked about. It was a time of Crusades, knights and tales of chivalry. Among the key words of courtly love were courtesy, nobility, affability, joy, gentleness and unity of spirit. These ideals were not well lived out as history shows, but they remained very real ideals for Francis and Clare. Another important feature of this period was the use of ordinary language instead of Latin. This was a cultural shift which helped shape the world we live in.

From the historical sources there doesn't appear to be any meeting of the two when they were young. The war between Perugia and Assisi would have put paid to this. Clare was introduced into the way of prayer and of the Spirit by her mother (Lg C 3-4). We are told that during these early years Clare was inflamed with the Holy Spirit who moulded her inner self (Lg C 3). The love of God was poured into her heart by the Spirit (Rom. 5:5). Clare "bore a compassionate attitude" and she was kind "towards the miseries of the destitute" (Lg C4). Francis wished to follow Christ. He wished to be led by the Holy Spirit. St. Clare in her Testament speaks of the Cross that spoke to Saint Francis in San Damiano. "In fact almost immediately after his conversion, when the young man did not yet have brothers or companions, while building the church of San Damiano, where he was totally visited by divine consolation and impelled to abandon the world completely through great joy and the enlightenment of the Holy Spirit, the holy man made a prophecy about us that the Lord later fulfilled." (Test Cl, 10-11). Francis had a vision that the church of San Damiano would have a community of women.

Clare's family returned to Assisi in 1210 and Clare heard of the poverty and holiness of Francis. She came to know him and decided to become of his followers. He mediated Christ to her. For Clare and the medieval world Jesus was seen as mother (see Bynum, *Jesus as Mother*, 1982). In this light we understand Clare's vision of Francis as mother (see Proc 3:29 and Proc 6:13).

Francis showed Clare the way to Jesus. There grew a bond of affection between them. People often ask was there attraction between them. In all probability there was but in the words of Saint Exupery they looked together in the same direction. Their first love was God. Both contemplated the cross of San Damiano and were infused with the Holy Spirit. The Legend of Saint Clare tells us of the first encounter of Clare with Francis.

Hearing of the then celebrated name of Francis,
who, like a new man,
was renewing with new virtues
the way of perfection forgotten by the world,
she was moved by the Father of the spirits
– Whose initiatives each one had already accepted
although in different ways –
and immediately desired to see and hear him.
No less did he desire to see and speak with her,
impressed by the widespread fame of so gracious a young lady,
so that, in some way,
he, who was totally longing for spoil
and (who) had come to depopulate the kingdom of the world,
would be also able to wrest this noble spoil from the evil world and win her for his Lord.
He visited her and she more frequently him, moderating the times of their visits so that this divine pursuit could not be perceived by anyone nor objected to by gossip. For, with only one close companion accompanying her, the young girl, leaving her paternal home, frequented the clandestine meetings with the man of God, whose words seemed to her to be on fire and whose deeds were seen to be beyond the human.
The Father Francis encouraged her to despise the world,
showing her by his living speech
how dry the hope of the world was
and how deceptive its beauty.

He whispered in her ears of a sweet espousal with Christ,
persuading her to preserve the pearl of her virginal purity
for that blessed Spouse Whom Love made man.

(Legend of St. Clare, 5).

Clare eventually settled in San Damiano and came to know the love of God poured into her heart by the Holy Spirit. She chose Francis as her guide in her journey to God (Legend, 6). It is clear in the relationship that there was a genuine affection. In the Legend of Clare we hear speak of spiritual favours. She experienced being one in Spirit (see Lg C 45). In his biography of Saint Francis Celeno emphasises that "one and the same Spirit had led the brothers and then those little poor ladies out of this world" (2 Cel 204). The Holy Spirit used the I-Thou relationship of Francis to lead them both to a more profound I-Thou relationship with God. The Convent grew. Clare tells us that she proved to Francis that she and those who came to join her were able for this way of life. She says: "When the blessed Francis saw, however, that although we were physically weak and frail, we did not shun deprivation, poverty, hard work, trial or the shame or contempt of the world... he greatly rejoiced in the Lord" (Test C 27). She tells the sisters "and loving one another with the love of Christ may you demonstrate without in your deeds the love you have within" (Test C 59). One of St. Paul's favourite terms for living in the power of the Holy Spirit is to say one is "in Christ." The life of the little community is said to be "in Christ."

In Clare's rule (Reg CIII, 12-14) she tells the sisters to receive communion more often than was the norm. This shows us the way the Spirit worked. It was through the daily routine of silence, liturgical prayer (the office and the Eucharist), meditation and the work they have been given to do. It is love that the Spirit worked quietly and gently like the gentle breeze where Elijah met God (1 Kings 19:9-18). Clare radiated compassionate love and her fame spread far beyond her little convent.

In her Testament she tells us the sisters to look at the figure of Jesus. He is the word made flesh and the word is love for us. This love means we are loved and accepted in a pure way. This is the source and inspiration of her life and her sisters:

Out of love for the God Who was placed poor in the crib, lived poor as in the world, and remained naked on the cross, may (the Lord Cardinal) always have his little flock, which the Lord Father has begotten in His holy Church by the word and example of our blessed father Francis by following the poverty and humility of His beloved Son and His glorious Virgin Mother, observe the holy poverty that we have promised to God and our most blessed father Saint Francis. And may he always encourage and support them in these things.

(Test C 45ff).

This is the love Clare contemplated daily and in the power of the Spirit this is what transformed her.

Clare and her sisters

They entered each in their union but yet in communion with each other into a deep I-Thou relationship with Jesus in the love of the Holy Spirit. Clare tells Agnes of Prague:

> "...as a pure virgin
> embrace the poor Christ.
> Look upon him who became contemptible for you
> and follow him...
> Most noble Queen,
>   gaze,
>   consider,
>   contemplate,
>   desiring to imitate you
>   spouse"

(2L Ag 11f).

There again we hear the language of the Song of Songs in expressing the love between the soul and God. She calls Jesus the spouse - the bridegroom of the Song of Songs. She goes on to say to Agnes:

"If you suffer with Him you shall rejoice with Him,
Weeping with Him you will rejoice with Him:
dying on the cross of tribulation with Him,
you will possess the Heavenly mansions with Him."

(2 Lg 21).

Clare alludes to the Letter to the Romans here. Paul says in the Letter to the Romans:

"I think what we suffer in this life can never be compared to the glory as yet unrevealed, which is waiting for us. The whole of creation is eagerly waiting for God to reveal his children."

(Romans 8:18f).

Paul is telling us that while we may suffer now our prayer is that of Jesus for the healing of the world. He calls us to work with him in the Spirit to help heal the world. This is why Clare tells Agnes that "we will rejoice." In the words of the movements of the sixties: "We shall overcome."

In looking at Paul himself we get an insight into Clare's experience. Paul described his I-Thou encounter. He invoked the verb "to reveal" (Apokalytein: Galatians 1:16) for the noun "revelation" (Apokalysis: Galatians 1:2; 2 Cor. 12:7). Both words capture the sense of what he experienced as outside of himself and not something that he had produced. He saw God revealed in Jesus and he experienced the love of God in Jesus. In Galatians 1:15-16 Paul speaks that God was "pleased to reveal his son in me ('en emoi')". He is now one with Christ. Later in the letter he says: "I have been crucified with Christ and I live now not with my own life but with the life of Christ who lives in me. The life I now live in this body I live in faith: faith in the son of God who loved me and gave himself for me." (Gal. 2:20). Paul's experience of meeting the risen Jesus transformed him and he became one with Christ. Clare, Francis, Seraphim, and so many others meet the risen Jesus in the Spirit and find their lives "in Christ." Clare is like Paul in that she too is in union with Jesus and by her compassionate love and gentle ways showed (or as Paul said revealed) the compassionate Christ.

In the letter to the Romans Paul says:

> So then, brothers and sisters, we are debtors, not to the
> flesh, to live according to the flesh – for if you live
> according to the flesh, you will die; but if by the Spirit you
> put to death the deeds of the body, you will live. For all who
> are led by the Spirit of God are children of God. For you did
> not receive a spirit of slavery to fall back into fear, but you
> have received a spirit of adoption. When we cry, "Abba!
> Father!" it is that very Spirit bearing witness with our spirit
> that we are children of God, and if children, then heirs, heirs
> of God and joint heirs with Christ – if, in fact, we suffer
> with him so that we may also be glorified with him.
>
> (Rom. 8:12-17).

The vital dynamism of the Spirit constitutes our adoption as children of
God. We call God "Abba" as Jesus did. We are now joint heirs with
Christ. The one who follows Jesus in the Spirit and destined in one day
to share with Jesus in glory. Looking "unto Jesus" we see our hope of
our resurrection and peace with God. Our union with Jesus and his call
to each of us to be the people he has called us to be leads us to the hope
that all people will be saved. Not just all people but the entire creation
(Rom. 8:18-25). However now in the inbetween times between the
beginning of the new creation in the risen Jesus and the ultimate
consummation of all things we have to face suffering. However, we are
in communion with Jesus who overcame the world (see Jn 16:33). He
has left us his Spirit as a reassurance that we too will overcome and find
peace in him some day. The Spirit is the empowering presence of God
in our world.

> Likewise the Spirit helps us in our weakness; for we do not
> know how to pray as we ought, but that very Spirit
> intercedes with sighs too deep for words. And God, who
> searches the heart, knows what is the mind of the Spirit,
> because the Spirit intercedes for the saints according to the
> will of God.

We know that all things work together for good for those
who love God, who are called according to his purpose.

(Rom. 8:22-28).

The Spirit is the downpayment or guarantee of the revelation that is yet
to come. (e.g. 2 Cor. 1:22; 5:5; Eph. 1:14). The Spirit works deep in our
hearts in our innermost being. Only God fully understands the language
and mind of the Spirit and recognises that Spirit assisted prayer is of the
mind of God. It is part of God's faithfulness that the Spirit would play a
part in the prayers of the Christian. Even when things go wrong for us
God works with those who love him to produce good. We are not alone.
Clare witnessed to Paul's words in her life as did Francis and Seraphim
in their own ways. They all witness to the truth of Paul's words. God is
always faithful (e.g. see 1 Th. 5:24)[1].

Kierkegard compared praying to "respiration", breathing. In the O.T. the
word for spirit is ruach. This can mean "wind" or "breath". Praying in
the Spirit is as important or more important. This is then healthy for the
body. The following incident in Clare's life shows us that she lived in
this way. She had become a living "prayer".

How She Cured Sister Andrea of Her Scrofula

The witness also said that when one of the sisters, Sister
Andrea da Ferrara, was suffering from a scrofula in her
throat, Lady Clare knew by inspiration she was very
tempted by her desires for a cure. One night, while Sister
Andrea was below in the dormitory, she squeezed her throat
with her own hands so strongly she lost her voice. The holy
mother knew this through the Spirit. Then she immediately
called the witness, who slept near her and told her. "Go
down immediately to the dormitory because Sister Andrea
is seriously ill; boil an egg and give it to her to swallow.
After she has recovered her speech, bring her to me." And
so it was done. When the Lady asked Sister Andrea what

---

[1]This is developed by N.T. Wright in his work "Paul and the Faithfulness of God" (London,
2013).

had been the matter, Sister Andrea did not want to tell her. Then the attentive Lady told her everything in detail as it had happened. And this spread about among the sisters.

(Process 3:16).

Clare's discernment of Andrea's distress is a gift of God. It seems that Andrea suffered from tuberculosis and it was late at night. Clare tells Sister Filippa to go and give Andrea an egg. It shows again how God works in the ordinary. Andrea seems to have been of a nervous disposition. Clare deals gently with her and brings her to health. She loves her back to life. Her gentleness and compassion are signs of the action of the Spirit.

St. Bonaventure and the Holy Spirit

St. Bonaventure was born in Bagnoregio, near Orvieto, in 1217. As a young child he was very ill. His mother prayed to Saint Francis and he was cured (Lg M, prol. 3). And he grew to study at the University of Paris. The thirteenth century saw the growth of the university. One of his teachers was Alexander of Hales who influenced Bonaventure and he entered the Franciscan Order. He became a master of theology in Paris. The order was tearing itself asunder at this stage and in the eye of this storm Bonaventure became Minister-General. He tried to bring the differing factions of the order together. Ewert Cousins said that Bonaventure's work is like a gothic cathedral. The two main towers of the Cathedral are the Trinity and Christ, which join together the flying buttresses of humanity and creation. There is no Trinity without Christ and no Christ without Trinity. (Ewert Cousins *Coincidence of Opposites* p.49).

Distressed by all he had to do he went to pray at La Verna where Francis had received the wounds of Christ, the stigmata. Then it came to his mind that this was Francis' rapture in contemplation and one had to follow him in the love of the crucified one (Journey of the Soul into God, prologue 3). Francis became important in his writings because he showed in his being the action of the Holy Spirit and he became a true image of the crucified one. He led Bonaventure, as he had Clare to contemplate the figure of Jesus. Bonaventure's aim is described in the following way: "undaunted, together with all the saints, you may know the length and breadth, height and depth of the love of Christ which surpasses all knowledge, so that you may be filled with the fulness of God" (Eph. 3:18-19). There is no way to God "than through the most loving love of the crucified" (Journey, Prol. 2).

Bonaventure sees the Father as the source of all and supreme goodness. This goodness is always self-diffusing. The Trinity of goodness reveals itself as a unity of persons, "beings-in love". The one called Father is the source of all and gives himself to all. We may refer to the term "kenosis" – emptying himself in the sense he gives all away. He expressed himself in "generating" another person ("generating" is metaphorical in the sense that there was never a time when the son did not exist). "Word" is the term favoured by Bonaventure for the son. The eternal ideas of the Father are expressed in the Word. He is the archetype of all things that are. In him we are as if "God's little words." The significance of the "Word" as expression of the Father's self-diffusive goodness is borne out in the idea that through the Word the Father creates. The Word can be seen as the Father's ideas expressed. Jesus is the "Word made flesh" (Jn. 1:14). The Holy Spirit proceeds from the mutual love between the Father and Son. Bonaventure will describe the Spirit as the perfect act of the divine will. As the fruit of mutual love the Spirit is gift. God is love and the perfection of love is found in loving. Loving is perfected in giving. The Spirit is the bond of love between Father and Son and he makes active the reciprocal love between Father and Son. The Father and the Son love us in the Spirit and the Spirit comes to us to bring us into the love relationship between Father and Son.

Compassion is an expression of love and it helps mark out those who live in the Spirit. The word compassion is derived from the Latin words 'passio' and 'cum' and together they mean "to suffer with". Compassion is seen in the figure of Jesus, the Word made flesh. Jesus expresses the infinite compassion of God for all people. He enters the places of pain of our world. He shares in our brokenness, fear, confusion and anguish. He mourned with those who were lonely and wept with those in tears. Compassion means full immersion in the condition of being human. In one of his meditations Bonaventure wrote:

O My God, good Jesus,
Although I am in every way without merit and unworthy,
Grant to me, who did not merit to be present
At these events in the body, that I may ponder them
Faithfully in my mind and experience toward you,
My God crucified and put to death for me,
That feeling of compassion.

        (The Tree of Life in Cousins, *Bonaventure*, p.158).

The Spirit leads us to imitate Jesus. Invite men to come to be like the beloved, to become loving compassionate beings. That is what we are called to be to become fully human. We are called to become totally dependent on God (Francis and Clare), to be radically turned towards God and to be transformed into beings of total love.

Writing to a Poor Clare nun Bonaventure says:

> Your heart is the altar of God. It is here that the fire of intense love must burn always. You are to feed it every day with the wood of the cross of Christ and the commemoration of his passion.... Let your love lead your steps to Jesus wounded, to Jesus crowned with thorns... there transformed into Christ by your burning love for the Crucified... transfixed by the sword of intimate compassion, seek nothing, desire nothing, wish for no consolation other than to be able to die with Christ on the cross. Then you may cry out with the Apostle Paul: With Christ, I am nailed to the cross. It is now no longer I that live, but Christ lives in me.
>
>   (Perf. ist 6:2)

This is the work of the Holy Spirit. Becoming like Christ is about where the centre of our lives is located, how receptive we are to God's love and, in turn, how we share love with others. The example of Christ crucified shows us the need to cling to God in faith and place our absolute trust in him alone. The last word is not the cross of suffering of love but the victory of love which Jesus wins for us in his suffering and death. (Leg M 13.5). Relationship to God, who is by nature self-giving love allows Bonaventure to describe the restoration of the human image in Christ as a restoration in compassionate love. By turning to God through the crucified in love, Francis was a man transformed. Bonaventure in the Legenda Maior (the major life of St. Francis) describes Francis in the following way:

> True piety,
> which according to the Apostle
> gives power to all things,
> had so filled Francis's heart
> and penetrated its depths
> that it seemed to have claimed the man of God
> completely into its dominion.
> This is what,
> through devotion, lifted him up into God;
> through compassion, transformed him into Christ;
> through self-emptying, turned him to his neighbour;
> through universal reconciliation with each thing,
> refashioned him to the state of innocence.
>
> (Legenda Maior, 6:1)

What is said of Francis is true of Clare. She, through compassion, was transformed into Christ, through self-emptying towards her neighbour. Her expression of being transformed complements that of Francis. Through their mutual interaction in the Spirit they enabled each other to be transformed in God. Jacapone da Todi (+1306) was an Italian Franciscan from Umbria in the 13th century. He wrote several laudi (songs in praise of God) in Italian, the vernacular. He was one of the earliest pioneers in Italian theatre. He dramatised Gospel subjects. He was a troubled person in troubled times. In talking of Clare's compassion he gives life to our more general ideas of compassion. He says:

> "Among others, Saint Clare came,
> Bringing with her, her sisters:
> Greedy for such treasures she tried in vain
> to pull out these nails with her teeth.
>
> (Laud 61, *St. Francis and the Seven Icons of the Cross*)

This laud is dedicated to St. Francis' reception of the stigmata. Jacopone sees Francis as another Christ. Clare is filled with compassion for the crucified one. The treasures she is "greedy for" is the final victory of love. Jacope uses a strong expression to show the passion of Clare's love – she tries to pull out the nails with her teeth!

Chapter 8

Journeying into God:
The Resumed Conversation

Compassion means loving totally. This is what Jesus did. He entered into the world of sin and division and alienation. He entered this alienation and ended it by his death and resurrection. Through his death and resurrection he opened a new order, a new creation. In him we find love, acceptance and forgiveness. This is not the experience many have. Zampano, in the film La Strada, was brutal. People like him had been brutalised and they responded with brutality. Gelsomina was gentle and loving as a child, but in the face of a world that is evil she feels worthless. The love they have for each is overcome by Zampano's brutality. We can see Christ's sufferings in these characters. He suffered out of compassion for people like Zampano and Gelsomina to heal them and indeed all of us. Clare joined him in this. She became a witness to his loving compassion. He offered love but was rejected. This was not the end. Love proved as strong as death and he was returned to life. He sent his Spirit so we could share in his triumph over death.

Thérèse of Lisieux was at one time full of fear and scruples. She had to come to love and accept herself. She faced her own mixed emotions and pettiness. Part of her poverty was to be able to love herself as she was. She suffered her own powerlessness until she discovered her vocation – to be love in the heart of the Church. She surrendered to this love. When she could be gentle with her own weaknesses – true sanctity, she said, was to bear patiently our own weaknesses – then she could be gentle with others. Clare, in her own way, came to know herself as she was. She, too, surrendered to love and her source of strength wasn't herself but the love of God poured into her heart. She bore witness to this and when she found peace, many were drawn to her and found peace.

The Father

God is love. His love is greater than our love and indeed our love is rooted in him because he created us. He loves us and gave his only Son for us. How do we think of the Father? The first thing is the term Father – God transcends the category of maleness. In Gen. 1:26 we see that both maleness and femaleness together form the image of God. We are not meant to be alone. God is greater than our maleness and femaleness. In the book of Exodus we see that God is "a God of tenderness and compassion, slow to anger, rich in kindness and faithfulness" (Ex. 34:6). This is who God is and this statement is the act of faith of God's people. Here God uses the term rehem, the Hebrew word for compassion. The word itself comes from the idea of womb. God is as much Mother as Father. In the prophet Isaiah we hear God say:

> "Does a woman forget her baby at the breast
> or fail to cherish the son of her womb.
> Yet even if these forget
> I will never forget you" (Is. 49:15)

God is Father with a maternal heart. Our words can never reach the depths of God. This is the God Jesus reveals to us. He tells us "The Father and I are one" (Jn. 10:30). He tells us later "As the Father has loved me so I love you" (Jn. 15:9). Philip asks Jesus to let him see the Father and Jesus tells him that he is in the Father and the Father is in him. (see Jn. 19:8-11). God raised Jesus from the dead (e.g. 1 Con. 15:1-34). He has inaugurated a new generation of which we are part (see Acts 13:22-33). We are given a new destiny. Peter says in his letter: "Blessed be God the Father of our Lord Jesus Christ who in his great mercy has given us a new birth as his children, by raising Jesus Christ from the dead so that we have a sure hope, and the promise of an inheritance that can never be spoilt or soiled and never fade away" (1 Pt. 1:3). Later he says (echoing Is. 52:13-53:12) "through his wounds you have been healed" (1 Pt. 2:24). Through the Spirit we are invited to share in the divine I-Thou relationship.

The Father in Von Balthasar

Hans Urs Von Balthasar has reflected on Jesus' revelation to us of the love of God, the one he calls Father. In Jesus we see that the kingdom of God is already "in the midst of you" (Lk. 17:21) and "has come upon you" (Mt. 12:28; Mk. 2:19). In the prologue of John's Gospel we hear that the Word was with God in the beginning (Jn. 1:2). In the original Greek the suggestion is that the word was with God as a child at the breast. This is the God Jesus, the word made flesh, revealed to us.

> According to Jesus Christ's own portrayal of himself... (he proffers) himself consistently as the definitive "interpretation" (cf. Jn 1:18) of God the Father: the Father has not disappeared into Jesus Christ; the Father remains the point of reference from whom Christ comes; on this basis he speaks and acts; he takes his bearings from the Father; and it is to him that he returns. Jesus wants to be understood as "the truth" only in this context, that is, as the Father's perfect unveiling and manifestation in the Son.
>
> (TD 3, p.506 see also GL1, p.189)

Jesus, according to Von Balthasar is simultaneously the Father's self-expression and is at the same time the one who empties himself, taking the form of a slave (Ph. 2:5-7). The idea here is one of kenosis. This means he gives everything of himself to the Father and in the mission God has given him he becomes fully who he is called to be.

Von Balthasar coined the term "Theodroma" to express God's activity in the world. Our life is not static but dramatic. The same is true of God. Drama is a better way of expressing God's love, and the word Von Balthasar used to help us grasp God's ways in Theodrama. "The Cross appears as the centre and zenith of the theodramatic action" (TD3, p.60). The First Epistle of John provides us with the following insight: "God is love. God's love was revealed in our midst in this way: he sent his only Son to the world" (1 Jn. 4:8f) and "the way we came to understand love was that he laid down his life for us" (1 Jn. 3:16). Von Balthasar emphasises the 'obedience' of Jesus, yet this qualification is important:

The application of the concept of obedience to the divine Person is, of course, a figure of speech – an anthropomorphism. But, in the final analysis, all human speech about God is anthropomorphic, and this figure has been made definitive and proper by the incarnation of the Son (Phil 2:7). In applying it, everything is to be excluded from the concept of obedience that derives from the relationship between God and the creature insofar as the creature is regarded qua creature, that is, as having its original in nothingness. Everything is to be retained, on the other hand, and translated into the infinite (in the sense of the via eminentiae) that pertains to the analogy between God and the creature as the positive image of God, or more properly, of the Trinity. The obedience of which the Son of God gave us an example in his human nature is by no means merely something that is grounded in his human nature... Like all his utterances, it is not only borne by his divine Person; it is also a positive revelation of his divine Person – and hence of his divine nature – translated into human terms.

(Esl, p.7 cf TD3 p.181).

In speaking of God the Father Von Balthasar uses the term "Pathos", this is the suffering of love. He borrowed the term "pathos" from Abraham Heschel.

God raised Jesus on the third day by the power of the Holy Spirit and sent the Spirit among us at Pentecost. We are called to be one with son turned towards the Father. It is in burning love for the crucified and risen one that we enter this place – in this we find peace.

Clare and the Way:

Clare was in love with the crucified and risen one. In her rule she speaks of poverty - the absolute trust one should have as a child of God. The essence of Clare's life is the love of a person – Jesus Christ. Her life was a response to his love: "She wanted to have nothing but Christ the Lord." (Lg C 13). Her spirituality is "Jesus": "The Son of God has become for us the Way that our blessed Father Francis, his true lover and imitator, has shown us and taught by example" (Test C 5).

The death of Jesus was an object of profound meditation for Clare. Almost every day she would have seen the San Damiano cross. She tells Agnes of Prague:

> "But as a poor virgin
> embrace the poor Christ.
> Look upon Him Who became contemptible for you,
> and follow Him, making yourself contemptible in this world for Him.
> Most noble Queen,
>   gaze,
>   consider,
>   contemplate
>   desiring to imitate Your Spouse.
> (Who) though more beautiful than the children of men became, for your salvation, the lowest of men, was despised, struck, scourged untold times throughout His entire body, and then died amid the suffering of the Cross.
> If you suffer with Him, you will reign with Him.
> weeping with Him, you will rejoice with Him;
> dying on the cross of tribulation with Him,
> you will possess heavenly mansions with Him
> among the splendour of the saints
> and in the Book of Life your name will be called glorious among the peoples."
>
> (2 LAg 20-22)

This is a theme picked up again and again in Clare's world (e.g. see Test C 45; Proc 10:3, 10:10, 11:2,3).

> "Once, the day of the most sacred Supper arrived, in which the Lord loved His own until the end. Near evening, as the agony of the Lord was approaching, Clare, sad and

afflicted, shut herself up in the privacy of her cell. While in her own prayer she was accompanying the praying Saviour and when saddened even to death she experienced the effect of His sadness, she was filled at once with the memory of His capture and of the whole mockery and she sank down on her bed. All that night and the following day, she was so absorbed that she remained out of her senses. She seemed to be joined to Christ and to be otherwise totally insensible always focusing the light of her eyes on one thing."

(Leg C, 31)

Here we see Clare's communion with Jesus. She becomes prayer. The legend tells us:

"Truly dead to the flesh
she was thoroughly a stranger to the world,
continually occupying her soul
with sacred prayers and divine praises.
She had already focused
the most fervent attention of her entire desire on the Light
and she opened more generously the depths of her mind
to the torrents of grace
that bathe a world of turbulent change."

(Legend of Clare, 19).

Clare's intercession brought healing to many. Only a few were recorded at the Process of Canonisation. At her intercession the Saracens left San Damiano (Leg C 21-22) and in the following year Assisi was spared destruction (Leg C 23). She shows us the way to the peace that comes from a loving relationship with God, the shalom of which the Hebrew bible speaks.

The Prayer of Jesus

Clare's prayer (and our prayer) is rooted in the prayer of Jesus. In the Gospel of Mark we see Jesus praying at different times (e.g. 1:35 and 6:46). Jesus always looks towards God his Father. He calls the Father by a personal name "Abba" and he brings us (if we wish) to a relationship with God in which we can call him 'Abba' (Rom. 8:14-17 and Gal. 4:6). In Luke's Gospel Jesus often goes away to pray in solitude to 'Abba' especially before making decisions (e.g. Lk. 6:12f).

Jesus' prayer is at once the prayer of a son and the prayer of a servant, the suffering servant. In the garden of Gethsemane Jesus says: "...let it be as you would have it, not I" (Mk. 14:36). We can be prone to be too literal in interpretation of obedience. Jesus' will and the Father's will were one – we use the term 'obedience' to try and express the mystery of Jesus wrestling with his fate in Gethsemane. The word obedience itself comes from the Latin "Ob" and "Audire" - from "hearing". Jesus has to discern God's will and this is seen in the Gethsemane scene.

Mark's account of Gethsemane goes as follows:

> They came to a small estate called Gethsemane, and Jesus said to his disciples, 'Stay here while I pray'. Then he took Peter and James and John with him. And a sudden fear came over him, and great distress. And he said to them, 'My soul is sorrowful to the point of death. Wait here, and keep awake.' And going on a little further he threw himself on the ground and prayed that, if it were possible, this hour might pass him by. 'Abba (Father)!' he said 'Everything is possible for you. Take this cup away from me. But let it be as you, not I, would have it.' He came back and found them sleeping, and he said to Peter, 'Simon, are you asleep Had you not the strength to keep awake one hour? You should be awake, and praying not to be put to the test. The spirit is willing, but the flesh is weak.' Again he went away and prayed, saying the same words. And once more he came back and found them sleeping, their eyes were so heavy; and they could find no answer for him. He came back a third time and said to them, 'You can sleep on now and take your rest. It is all over. The hour has come. Now the Son of Man is to be betrayed into the hands of sinners. Get us! Let us go! My betrayer is close at hand already.'
>
> (Mk. 14:32-42)

Mark uses the Greek words "ekthambeisthai" and "odokomein" to describe Jesus' condition. The words show Jesus in profound distress and agony of mind. He enters into a silent dialogue with God. He asks those with him to watch and pray but they sleep. In the silence Jesus comes to realise what the will of God is and he surrenders to this will: "let it be done as you would have it."

Paul describes Jesus' going in the hymn in the Letter to the Philippians:

> His state was divine,
> yet he did not cling
> to his equality with God
> but emptied himself
> to assume the condition of a slave,
> and became as men are;
> and being as all men are,
> he was humbler yet,
> even to accepting death,
> death on a cross.
> But God raised him high
> and gave him the name
> which is above all other names
> so that all beings
> in the heavens, on earth and in the underworld,
> should bend the knee at the name of Jesus
> and that every tongue should acclaim
> Jesus Christ as Lord,
> to the glory of God the Father.
>
> (Phil. 2:5-11).

Paul says of his own mission in Christ:

> But because of Christ, I have come to consider all these advantages that I had as disadvantages. Not only that, but I believe nothing can happen that will outweigh the supreme advantage of knowing Christ Jesus my Lord. For him I have accepted the loss of everything, and I look on everything as

so much rubbish if only I can have Christ and be given a place in him. I am no longer trying for perfection by my own efforts, the perfection that comes from the Law, but I want only the perfection that comes through faith in Christ, and is from God and based on faith. All I want is to know Christ and the power of his resurrection and to share his sufferings by reproducing the pattern of his death. That is the way I can hope to take my place in the resurrection of the dead. Not that I have become perfect yet: I have not yet won, but I am still running, trying to capture the prize for which Christ Jesus captured me. I can assure you my brothers, I am far from thinking that I have already won. All I can say is that I forget the past and I strain ahead for what is to come.

(Phil. 3:7-14).

St. Bonaventure (+1273)

Bonaventure's journey is as what McGinn calls, a "dying into love" (Bernard McGinn, *The Flowering of Mysticism*, p.110). In his "Journey of the Mind into God" (*Itinerarium Mentis in Deum*) he describes how he went to La Verna there to seek peace. As he prayed the image of the Seraph that imprinted the marks of the crucified on St. Fancis he meditated on God and his traces in our world. By looking at God's traces he is lifted up to meditate on the human person. He tells us God is closer to us than we are to ourselves (after Augustine). Then he is led to meditate on God he comes to meditate on Christ's death. Here we understand McGinn's expression "dying into love" because it is when we surrender ourselves to God that we truly come to life. Bonaventure says:

> "With Christ crucified
> let us pass out of this world to the Father
> so that when the Father is shown to us
> we may say with Philip:
> It is enough for us."

(See Cousins, *Bonaventure*, p.116)

Conclusion

The story of the prophet Elijah helps me see the journey we have been on. He had just overcome the prophets of Ba'al but Jezebel turned her anger against him. In his exile in the desert he cried to God: "Yahweh", he said "I have had enough. Take my life." (1 Kgs 19:3). Yahweh made him rest and eat to recover his strength. This is what St. Clare did with troubled souls.

Elijah continued on his journey to Mount Horeb. There he waited to experience the presence of God. The cave is a place where many people over the ages go to pray and experience solitude. The early desert fathers did this.

> There he went into the cave and spent the night in it. Then the word of Yahweh came to him saying, 'What are you doing here, Elijah?' He replied, 'I am filled with jealous zeal for Yahweh Sabaoth, because the sons of Israel have deserted you, broken down your altars and put your prophets to the sword. I am the only one left, and they want to kill me.' Then he was told, 'Go out and stand on the mountain before Yahweh'. Then Yahweh himself went by. There came a mighty wind, so strong it tore the mountains and shattered the rocks before Yahweh. But Yahweh was not in the wind. After the wind came an earthquake. But Yahweh was not in the earthquake. After the earthquake came a fire. But Yahweh was not in the fire. And after the fire there came the sound of a gentle breeze. And when Elijah heard this, he covered his face with his cloak and went out and stood at the entrance of the cave.
>
> (1 Kg 19:9-14)

He had now left the place of the desert – the desert also of his own limits and weaknesses. This also was the experience of the people Moses led through the desert.

Now at Horeb Elijah has to come to God (Yahweh) at a deeper and newer level. He discovers Yahweh in the gentle breeze. The hebrew word for the "gentle breeze" "demanãh" comes from the root DHM which means being still and remaining silent. It has the inner meaning of being empty for God. Clare and Francis represent the gentle breeze for me. They reflect the love of God and lead us to that place where we can let God in.

Leonard Cohen in his song *Anthem* said:

> "There is a crack in everything
> That's how the light gets in."

Clare let the light in and she radiated the light of love to the world. Her Italian name 'Chiara' refers to brightness.

Epilogue

The Legend of Saint Clare 45 tells us of the last hours of the Saint's life and tells us of her blessing the sisters of San Damiano. Her blessing is believed to be of the following form. Armstrong says that the tradition of the Poor Clares has always considered this blessing similar to the one given by St. Francis to Leo while they were at La Verna (The Lady, p.66)

> In the name of the Father and of the Son and of the Holy Spirit.
> May the Lord bless you and keep you.
> May He show His face to you and have mercy on you.
> May He turn His countenance to you and give peace to you, my sisters and daughters,
> and to all others who come and remain in your company and to others both now and in the future, who have persevered until the end in every other monastery of the Poor Ladies.
> I, Clare, a handmaid of Christ, a little plant of our most holy father Francis, a sister and mother of you and the other poor sisters, although unworthy, beg our Lord Jesus Christ through His mercy and the intercession of His most holy Mother Mary and of blessed Michael the Archangel and of all the holy angels of God, our our blessed father Francis, and of all men and women saints, that the heavenly Father give you and confirm for you this most holy blessing in heaven and on earth: on earth, by multiplying you in grace and His virtues among His servants and handmaids in His Church Militant; in heaven, by exalting you and glorifying you among His holy men and women in His Church Triumphant.
> I bless you during my life and after my death, as I am able, out of all the blessings, with which the Father or mercies has blessed and will bless His sons and daughters in heaven and on earth and a spiritual father and mother have blessed

and will bless their spiritual sons and daughters. Amen.

Always be lovers of your souls and those of all your sisters. And may you always be eager to observe what you have promised the Lord.

May the Lord always be with you and may you always be with Him. Amen.

Sources

Francis of Assisi: Early Documents, Vol I: The Saint. Edited by Regis J. Armstrong, Wayne Hellmann and William J. Short, New York, 1999.

Francis of Assisi: Early Documents, Vol II: The Founder. New York, 2000.

Francis of Assisi: Early Documents, Vol III: The Prophet. New York, 2001.

Clare of Assisi: Early Documents: The Lady. Translated and edited by Regis J. Armstrong. New York, 2006.

Fonti Francescane (FF in text), E. Caroli (ed.), Assisi, 2004.

Dizionario Francescano, E. Caroli (ed.), Padua, 2002.

Dizionario Bonaventuriano, E. Caroli (ed.), Padua, 2008.

Select Bibliography

F. Accroca, *Francesco e Chiara: In preghiera come meditazione del mistero dell'Incarnazione*. F. Sor (1998) 254-270.

M. P. Alberzoni, *Chiara e il papato,* Milan, 1995.

M. P. Alberzoni, *Clare of Assisi and the Poor Sisters in the Thirteenth Century,* New York, 2004.

G. Bini, *Chiara e Francesco: insieme nella sequela di Cristo in Come Chiara e Francesco,* Maria Chiaia and F. Incampo, Milan, 2007.

M. Bartoli, *Chiara d'Assisi,* Rome 1989.

C. W. Bynum, *Jesus as Mother,* California, 1982.

C. W. Bynum, *Holy Feast and Holy Fast,* London, 1987.

G. Casagrande, *Intorno a Chiara,* Assisi, 2011.

E. Cousins (ed.), *Bonaventure, Classics of Western Spirituality,* New York, 1978.

— *Bonaventure and the Coincidence of Opposites,* Chicago, 1978.

D. Covi, D. Dozzi (eds.) *Francescanesimo al femminile,* Rome, 1992.

C.G. Cremaschi, *Chiara donna della prerghiera,* VM 74 (2003) 441-462.

— *Il Cantico dei Cantici in Chiara d'Assisi,* VM 75 (2004) 39-51.

— *Chiara di Assisi, Un Silenzio che grida,* Assisi, 2009

I. Delio, *Simply Bonaventure,* New York, 2001.

— *Clare of Assisi: A Heart Full of Love,* New York, 2007.

R. Di Muro, *La Mistica Di Santa Chiara Assisi*, Rome, 2012.

C. Frugoni, *Una Solitudine Abitata. Chiara d'Assisi*, Bari, 2006.

L. Giacometti (ed.), *Dialoghi con Chiara d'Assisi*, Assisi, 1995.

M. Guida, *Una legenda in cerca d'autore*, Société Des Bollandistes, Brussels, 2010.

C. A. Lainati, *Santa Chiara d'Assisi*, Padua, 2008.

C. Leonardi, *Chiara d'Assisi in Agiografie Medievali*, A. Degl'Innocenti and F. Santi, Florence, 2011.

R. Manselli, *San Francesco d'Assisi*, Rome, 1980.

Ingrid J. Peterson, *Clare of Assisi: A Biographical Study*, New York, 1993.

A. Bartolomei Romagnoli, *Donne e Francescanesimo in Santitàe Mistica Femminile Nel Medioevo*, pp 215-311, Spoleto, 2013.

A. Bartolomei Romagnoli, *Per un Rilettera della Regola di Chiara d'Assisi Silenzio e Clausura* (email to author) – awaiting publication date 2013.

A. Rotzetter, *Il servizio negli scritti subordinazione o maturità* in D. Covi and D. Dozzi (eds.), *Chiara Francescanesimo al Feminile*, Bologna, 2004.

A. Rotzetter, *Klara von Assisi. Die Erste Fraziskanishe Frau*, Frieburg, 1993.

J. Saward, *The Mysteries of March*, London, 1980.

P. Tillich: *Systematic Theology* (3 vols.), New York, 1951-1958

– *The Courage to Be*, New York, 1952

– *The Shaking of the Foundations*, London 1949

O. Van Asseldonk, *Lo Spirito da Vita,* Rome, 1994.

H. U. Von Balthasar, *Mysterium Paschale,* Edinburgh, 1969.
                    The Glory of the Lord (7 vols), Edinburgh, 1982-1989.
                    Theodrama (5 vols), Edinburgh, 1988-1998.
                    Theo-logic (3 vols), Edinburgh, 2002-2005.

N. T. Wright, *Paul and The Faithfulness of God* (4 bks), London, 2013.

Printed in Great Britain
by Amazon